MW00564272

The *WITCH* of
THE MONONGAHELA

.

The WITCH of
THE MONONGAHELA

Folk Magic in Early Western Pennsylvania

Thomas White

THE
History
PRESS

Published by The History Press
Charleston, SC
www.historypress.com

Copyright © 2020 by Thomas White
All rights reserved

First published 2020

Manufactured in the United States

ISBN 9781467145152

Library of Congress Control Number: 2020938623

Notice: The information in this book is true and complete to the best of our knowledge. It is offered without guarantee on the part of the author or The History Press. The author and The History Press disclaim all liability in connection with the use of this book.

All rights reserved. No part of this book may be reproduced or transmitted in any form whatsoever without prior written permission from the publisher except in the case of brief quotations embodied in critical articles and reviews.

For my good friends Kurt, Ryan and Andy,
who appreciate the magic in a good story.

CONTENTS

ACKNOWLEDGEMENTS

Researching and writing this book required the help and support of many people. I want to thank my wife, Justina, and my children, Tom (who provided some illustrations) and Marisa, for their support and encouragement, as well as my brother Ed and my father, Tom. My mother, Jean, who passed away in 2011, instilled a curiosity in me at a young age about history and the unexplained and will always influence any project that I work on. Megan DeFries, Gerry O'Neil, Anaïs Grateau, Gina DelGreco Hertrick, Elisa Astorino, Kathleen Kenna, Fahmida Hossain and Elizabeth Williams all spent time proofreading and editing for me, and their input and suggestions are greatly appreciated. Maria Sholtis and Joan Peake from the Pennsylvania Room at the Uniontown Public Library and Marquel Sherry at the Indiana University of Pennsylvania Special Collections and Archives opened up their collections for me and provided important information. Author Sylvia Shults graciously provided information about Moll Derry's descendants and the tragic case of Rhoda Derry. I would also like to thank Lindsay Davenport, Brianna Brown, Michelle (Bertoni) McAndrew, Dr. Edward Brett, Dr. Joshua Forrest, Dr. Sara Baron, Tracie Ballock, Paula Toncheff, Kurt Wilson, Andy Grejda, Ryan Hughes, Vince Grubb, Brian McKee, Michael and Cassandra Witherel, Maggie Cervone and the staff of Coffee Buddha, who all helped in some way. In addition, this book would not have been possible without the work of the late George Swetnam, who dedicated many years to chronicling the region's unusual history.

INTRODUCTION

In the decades following the American Revolution, stories were told in the ancient hills and misty hollows of Fayette County, Pennsylvania, of a woman with mysterious powers. Rumors of magic surrounded her, and some locals believed that she could see into the future. As her reputation spread, desperate people came to the woman for healing and protection when they were ill or believed themselves to be cursed. Some were convinced that she could help find missing money, animals and belongings through her strange rituals. A few people even insisted that she could fly by some supernatural means. It was said that the strange woman slept in a large cradle with rockers that were aligned lengthwise, and by rocking herself she could launch into the air.

Moll Derry was her name, or at least that is what everyone called her. Her real name was Mary Derry (Moll is a diminutive form of Mary), and she lived in rural Georges Township near the small town of Haydentown, just south of the county seat of Uniontown. Derry's reputation was more ominous than that of a simple healer, however. Even though she was frequently helpful to those who came to her in need, Derry was not one to be angered or crossed. Local farmers who ended up on her bad side found that their cows would not produce milk and their bread would not rise. Her true enemies regretted being on the receiving end of her powers, and more than once, they ended up dead. It is not hard to imagine why, under such circumstances, Derry was associated with witchcraft. Over time, the enigmatic woman would come to be known as the Witch of the Monongahela because of her relative proximity to the important waterway. Others called her the Witch of the Little World, which was a nickname for her corner of the state. Her story would live on in Fayette County and the rest of southwestern Pennsylvania long after her death.

Witchcraft is not a subject that is usually associated with western Pennsylvania. Historians of the region, both professional and amateur, have traditionally focused on topics such as industrialization, labor, immigration, ethnicity and religion or events such as the French and Indian War and the Whiskey Rebellion. In America, historical witchcraft (as opposed to modern Neopagan practices) is more commonly linked with Salem and early colonial New England in the popular imagination. Yet states such as Pennsylvania, Maryland and West Virginia have far more accounts of witchcraft than Massachusetts. The primary difference is that the colonies/states south of New England did not execute witches, and therefore accounts attracted considerably less national attention. Pennsylvania's history is saturated with little-known accounts of folk magic and witchcraft. Virtually every county has at least one tale, and some have dozens. While researching my book *Witches of Pennsylvania: Occult History and Lore*—which is a brief survey of the history of witchcraft in the state—I was genuinely surprised at just how extensive the belief in witchcraft was and, in some cases, still is.

Since I am a native of the Pittsburgh region, I have always found the accounts of witches in the western part of the state interesting. I circled around the legend of Mary "Moll" Derry several times over the past twenty years while researching and writing about Pennsylvania's supernatural folklore. With each pass, I dug a little deeper into her story. The first accounts that I read were written in the mid-twentieth century by the prolific local writer/journalist/historian/folklorist George Swetnam. There was never any doubt that "Old Moll," as she was sometimes called, was a real flesh-and-blood woman. Her name and versions of her story appeared in various local history books, some dating back to a time when she existed in the living memory of the inhabitants of southern Fayette County. By all accounts, she lived for a long time, arriving in the county in the late 1700s and surviving far into the 1800s—certainly long enough to create a lasting influence in the lore of the region. As I delved further into the tales, I realized that even though there was some consistency in the accounts, much remained a mystery. Finally, I decided to attempt to compile everything that I had learned about Derry in one book. This volume is part biography, part an exploration of legends and part an examination of folk magic traditions. While there will always be a substantial amount of information that we will never know about Moll Derry, I will examine what we do know about her, her life and her legacy.

Derry has proven to be a complicated figure to assess. Though she has long been called a witch and was feared by many, most of the legends told about her also directly show or infer some level of respect. Historically, witches were often outsiders or people pushed to the fringes of society. They were viewed as dangerous individuals who tampered with unearthly forces and threatened social order. Derry, however, is often portrayed as a sort of dark hero in the legends. She curses murderers and thugs, finds lost items and warns a young woman of impending danger. These actions are more in line with her less ominous nickname "Fortune Teller of the Revolution." Still, there were those who assumed that her powers, whether used to heal, curse or see the future, had come from a pact with the devil.

To be properly understood, the Witch of the Monongahela must be put in her historical context. This includes two related but distinct lines of inquiry. The most straightforward of the two is finding factual historical data about her life and social and cultural environment. The second is more difficult because it involves examining how other writers have interpreted her over the past two centuries. With Old Moll, it is particularly difficult because of the limited available sources. As a woman living in a rural area in the late 1700s and early 1800s, the number of documents that she might appear in were few. Some early writers could rely on oral traditions when they created their own accounts, but those have been lost. Nevertheless, I have gathered every source that I could locate to create this historical account. There may very well be additional sources out there, but like a witch's familiar, they remain elusive.

I have laid out the parts of this book in an order that I believe tells the story of Moll Derry in the most comprehensive way. The first chapter is a brief retelling of the key legends involving Moll Derry as they are often repeated today. Once the reader is familiar with these tales, two chapters discuss beliefs about folk magic and witches in Pennsylvania. The actual mechanics and hands-on workings of folk magic will be explained. After that, we will take a slight detour, examining other cases of witchcraft in western Pennsylvania. This will provide a broader context in which to examine the legends relating to Old Moll. In the next chapter, we return to the story of Mary Derry, examining the scarce historic resources that can give us facts about her life. The following two chapters take a closer look at the legends of Moll Derry, examining how they developed over time and determining what parts of the tales can be historically verified. Finally, a brief conclusion reassesses the legends, and an epilogue tells the tragic and strange story of Derry's granddaughter Rhoda. For anyone who has read my previous

Gruss vom Hexentanzplatz
(Bodetal-Harz)

Central European traditions of witchcraft arrived in Pennsylvania with German immigrants. This antique postcard depicts witches gathering on a plateau in the Harz Mountains on Walpurgis Night. Similar traditions are linked to several Pennsylvania mountains. *Author's collection.*

book on historical witchcraft in Pennsylvania, there will be some familiar material in this volume. This is inevitable because it must be assumed that the reader will be new to the subject. However, there is a substantial amount of new information and analysis that I believe will be of interest to those with existing knowledge of the subject.

Fittingly, I am typing the final words to this introduction on Walpurgis Night (April 30). In central Europe, Walpurgis Night was celebrated before the feast of St. Walpurga on May 1. Ironically, one of the things St. Walpurga was invoked for was to protect against witchcraft. However, in German lore, Walpurgis Night also had another name—Hexannacht— or "Witches' Night." It was believed that witches gathered that night on Brocken Mountain, in the Harz Mountains and in the wilderness along the Elbe and Weser Rivers to hold black Sabbaths and consort with the devil and demons. It was a night both for witches and to stand against witches. The night's dual nature can be a metaphor for the legends of Old Moll Derry. Was she a misunderstood folk healer and fortune teller who helped people, or was she a witch who cursed her enemies and caused harm? Or was she perhaps both at the same time?

LEGENDS OF THE WITCH

Before we can begin our search for the historical Moll Derry, we first have to take a look at the legends and stories that are told about her. In a later chapter, I will examine these accounts in more detail and attempt to trace their development over the years. For now, however, I will merely synthesize and retell the most popular tales as they are repeated today so the reader is familiar with them. Most of the modern versions of the legends (including my own retellings) are based on the mid- and late twentieth-century writings of George Swetnam, who brought the stories to a wider audience in articles and books. Variations of these legends exist today in print and on the internet.

Since Derry lived a long time, physical descriptions of her changed over the years. She had always been a petite woman (which is why she could sleep in a cradle), but as time passed, she became more hag-like in the accounts, like a "traditional" witch—or at least what they are popularly imagined to be. As mentioned in the introduction, there were many who sought out Derry because of her skill at divining the future and finding lost money, items and animals. Swetnam wrote of one woman from Pittsburgh who visited her for help finding missing jewelry. Old Moll told the seeker that her neighbor had stolen the jewels, and sure enough, the neighbor confessed when accused. He also wrote of a farmer from Greene County who had misplaced a large amount of money. Derry directed him to look in his barn. It was there just as she said.

Of course, Derry was not always so friendly—at least in the stories. She could supposedly control rattlesnakes, which guarded her house from unwanted visitors. Any local farmer who foolishly crossed her could have problems with his livestock and crops, which could mean financial ruin. But there were those who fared even worse if Old Moll was not feeling merciful. There are four well-known accounts of Derry's wrath and the exercise of her magical powers that have been repeated over the years. These four accounts were not the only ones, but they are the most detailed and most popular. Together they form the core of the Moll Derry legend.

Sometimes Derry (or at least a witch believed to be Derry) was called by a different but similar name in the stories, like Moll Wampler, Moll Dell or Moll Pry. It has been asserted that people used a different name on occasion because the stories circulated while she was still alive, and they were afraid that they might anger her or her family. I will return to the issue of Derry's aliases later in the book. For now, let us examine the stories that gained her a fearsome reputation, beginning with the tale of three men who incurred her wrath one fateful day in the 1790s.

THE THREE HANGED MEN

The story of the three hanged men is perhaps the most frequently repeated legend about Old Moll. Her encounter with the men reportedly occurred either on the streets of Haydentown or in the countryside nearby in 1794 or 1795. Details are sparse, but for some reason, the men mocked Derry and her ability to see the future. After a few minutes, Derry turned and cursed the men, saying that they would all hang. Whatever reaction the three men had is not known. What is known is that it did not take very long for the first man to end up on the gallows.

Late in 1795, John McFall, in a drunken rage, killed a tavern keeper by tearing off the establishment's door, running him down and beating him with a club. He was convicted of murder and became the first man to be hanged in Fayette County. A few years later, a man named Ned Cassidy (or Casedy) helped rob and murder a peddler who was passing through the area. (In fact, the murder of the peddler would be central to another Derry story, which will be recounted shortly.) Cassidy left the area and went west into Ohio, where he ended up murdering a man in a bar fight. Before he went to the gallows there, he confessed to the murder of the

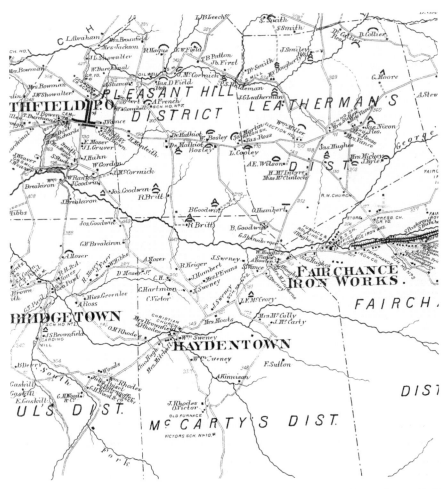

An 1872 map depicting the part of Fayette County around Moll Derry's former home. Basil Derry's property is marked in the bottom left corner of the map. *Author's collection.*

peddler in Fayette County. Finally, when the third man, who is usually unnamed, heard about Cassidy's hanging, he traveled to neighboring Greene County and hanged himself. The curse was seemingly fulfilled with his passing.

Sometimes other names—such as Butler, Dougherty and Flanagan—are given for the three men. Regardless, the story remains the same. The men, who all had bad reputations, mocked her and ended up dead.

THE MURDERED PEDDLER

Ned Cassidy's role in the disappearance and death of a peddler is a key part of another popular legend about Moll Derry. The story is sometimes said to have taken place around 1800 and other times the spring of 1818 or 1819. An unnamed peddler from New Jersey was traveling in Pennsylvania when he stopped at a tavern in Smithfield. There he met an old acquaintance by the name of John Updyke, who lived in the area. Updyke invited the man to stay at his home. He hesitantly agreed but admitted that he had also wished to get his fortune told by Moll Derry. The men left the tavern and met Updyke's friend Ned Cassidy along the way. Instead of taking the peddler to Moll Derry, Updyke and Cassidy led him out into the woods and murdered him, taking all of the money that he was carrying. The pair then dragged his body and dumped it into the pond at Ruble's Mill.

The following day, a man passing by found some blood on a post and in the woods near the pond. Soon the body was discovered as well. Though some members of the community suspected that Updyke and Cassidy were responsible for the man's death, there was no direct proof and no witnesses after they left the tavern. The two would never be arrested for the crime, but that does not mean that they got away with it.

In the days after the murder, Ned Cassidy began to feel a little guilty about what he had done. His conscience kept him up at night, so he decided that he would approach Moll Derry to ask if she had anything that would help him sleep. Even though he had previously mocked her, he knew of her alleged ability to heal and thought she could make him some kind of medicine or potion. When he visited Derry, she immediately said something like, "Why are you coming to me when your hands are still wet from your dirty work at the millpond?" As her cold and piercing eyes fell on him, he was startled and afraid. He quickly turned and walked away. As mentioned in the previous tale, not long after Cassidy left the area, he ended up dangling in a noose.

John Updyke's end would be much more painful. Around the time of the killing, there was another witch living near Updyke and the mill. Her name was Hannah Clarke, and it is commonly believed that she learned her magical skills from Moll Derry as her apprentice. One afternoon, not long after the murder, a prominent citizen named Valentine Moser paid a visit to Hannah Clarke. She showed him a rough drawing of Updyke that was on the back of her door. A nail was tapped into the door right where his head was drawn. The nail seemed to be tapped just once, as most of it still protruded from the door. Clarke explained to Moser that if she drove

An undated photo of Ruble's Mill. *Courtesy of the Pennsylvania Department of the Uniontown Public Library.*

the nail the entire way into the drawing, Updyke would die. Instead, she was tapping it in little by little so he would suffer for murdering the peddler.

His curiosity piqued, Moser decided to visit Updyke. Sure enough, he was complaining about a pain in his head. Moser revealed nothing of Clarke's curse to Updyke. As the weeks went by and the nail pushed ever so slowly into the drawing, Updyke's condition worsened. He could not sleep, remained bedridden and was afraid to be left alone. In a state of delirium, he finally admitted to killing the peddler when Moser visited again. When Hannah Clarke learned this, she drove the nail the rest of the way into the door, ending his life.

POLLY WILLIAMS AND THE WHITE ROCKS

The Witch of the Monongahela plays a role in another well-known tale from southwestern Pennsylvania. The tragic story of Polly Williams's death at the scenic White Rocks in Fayette County has been recounted numerous times over the past two centuries. Polly was an attractive young woman from New Salem. Her family was not wealthy, so she worked as a servant in the household of Jacob Moss to earn money. It was there that she met a young man named Philip Rogers, the son of Moss's wealthy neighbor. The two were immediately attracted to each other, and they began a romance that would last several years. Polly's family assumed that the two would get married, and when they moved west in 1808, Polly remained in Fayette County. Philip did propose to Polly but hesitated on making any definitive plans. Unfortunately for Polly, time passed, and despite Philip's promises, there was still no wedding. Perhaps Philip hesitated because of his higher social status and pressure from his own family.

Polly did not give up hope, but one day in 1810 while walking with a friend, she encountered Old Moll, sometimes referred to as Moll Pry in some published versions of the story. Derry/Pry warned the young woman that she should not go to the White Rocks with Rogers. Doing so would only lead to her death. The old witch foresaw Rogers hurling Polly down from the cliff onto the rocks below. Polly was shaken and disturbed by the encounter, and

An early twentieth-century postcard depicting the White Rocks in Fayette County. *Author's collection.*

she confided in Mrs. Moss for advice. Mrs. Moss, fearing for Polly's safety, encouraged her to call off the engagement and to stop seeing Rogers. Polly was unwilling to do so because she could not imagine her life without him.

Later that summer, Philip told Polly he was ready, and he sent for a minister to marry them. He told her to get her dress and meet him at the White Rocks. Polly's joy was stronger than her fear, and she ignored the warnings and followed Philip into the woods to the rocks. There was no minister, and no one knows for sure what transpired, but the next day, her body was found at the foot of the cliff. It appeared that she had been struck on the head with a rock before being pushed over the side. Philip was the prime suspect, of course, but his family was able to hire a prominent attorney from Pittsburgh, Senator James Ross. Rogers was acquitted and moved to Greene County to escape the public criticism. Polly was buried in Little White Rock Cemetery near Fairchance. To this day, people claim to see the ghost of Polly Williams at the White Rocks, forever waiting for Philip because she failed to heed the warning of Old Moll.

THE LOST CHILDREN OF THE ALLEGHENIES

The tragic story of the Lost Children of the Alleghenies is a well-known tale in Pennsylvania. As it takes place in April 1856, it is also the most recent legend chronologically that is associated with Moll Derry. In this tale, Derry allegedly goes by or is given the alias of Moll Wampler and plays a relatively minor role.

A late spring snowfall covered the Allegheny Mountains in Bedford County that year. Samuel and Susanna Cox lived with their three children in Spruce Hollow, near Pavia. Samuel was a hunter, and he was able to use the ample game in the region to provide for his family. On the morning after the snowfall, while the Cox family was eating breakfast, he heard his hunting dog barking outside. Samuel, believing that his dog had chased something up a tree, headed out with his rifle. Susanna, their two sons and their two-year-old daughter stayed inside and finished eating. While their mother was cleaning up, seven-year-old George and five-year-old Joseph slipped away and wandered outside, presumably to catch up with their father. When Susanna noticed they were gone, she assumed that they had done just that. What none of them realized was that Samuel had headed off deeper into the woods. The boys tried to follow but soon lost their way.

It was several hours before Samuel returned to the family cabin. Susanna expected to see the boys with him, but he was unaware that they had even left. A desperate panic set in as Samuel raced from the house to try to find the boys before nightfall. Susanna went to get neighbors to help in the search. They knew all too well the dangers that the boys faced alone in the cold forest, but no sign of them was found that day. As word of the missing boys spread, volunteers from surrounding communities and counties came to help with the search. Two weeks passed, and there was no sign of the boys. Some neighbors accused the couple of killing their own children and searched their cabin. Others thought the boys had been killed by a wild animal. Some of the searchers decided to seek out supernatural help as the search dragged on.

They knew of a woman with a reputation for witchcraft who could see the future and find lost items. She was called Moll Wampler, but many researchers and writers have believed that this was another case where the witch was actually Moll Derry, operating under or assigned an alias. The old woman lived alone in the mountains and used a scrying device called an Erdspiegel, which translated from German means "earth mirror." It worked like a crystal ball, allowing her to see past, present and future. When they visited Wampler, she placed the Erdspiegel in the bottom of a black bag and looked inside. After several minutes, she described a vague location where she saw the children. She claimed they were lying down on the mountain next to a large rock and some laurel beneath chestnut and rock oak trees. She thought they might be sleeping because she could see where they had chewed on mountain tea berries. After spending a few days searching for the spot, it was clear that Wampler had not given them the proper location. (In some versions, the angry locals beat or even kill Wampler for wasting their time.)

But in the end, the children were, in fact, discovered by a seemingly supernatural method. On the other side of the ridge, a young farmer named Jacob Dibert began having dreams of walking through the woods. In the dream, he first passed a dead deer. Not long after, he found a child's shoe. Then he came to a small stream, which he followed a short distance to a fallen tree. He saw the motionless figures of two young boys huddled near its roots. The dream disturbed Jacob, so he initially told only his wife about it. For the following two nights, Jacob had the exact same dream. Finally, he told his brother-in-law, Harrison Whysong, who was very familiar with the woods around Pavia. Though Harrison doubted that the dream meant anything, he believed he knew the area the Jacob described. One can imagine what they

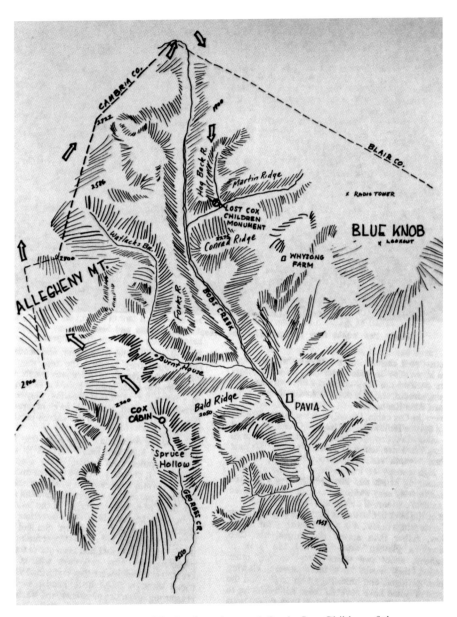

Map showing the area around Pavia where the search for the Lost Children of the Alleghenies took place. The route that the boys are believed to have taken is indicated with arrows. *Courtesy of the Bedford County Historical Society and Joe and Michelle McAndrew.*

Welcome To Cox Monument

The Cox children, George age 7, and Joseph age 5, wandered from their Spruce Hollow home on April 24, 1856. Hundreds of people searched for them for two weeks without success. Jacob Dibert, a local farmer, had the same dream three times about where the boys could be found. On May 8th Jacob and his brother in law, Harrison Whysong, set out to follow signs in his dream, a dead deer, a little shoe, a log across a stream and then a birch tree with a broken top. They found the boys bodies nestled in the roots of the birch. This monument marks the spot where the boys were found.

Jacob Dibert

The sign near the monument to the Cox boys that tells the story of how they were found because of Jacob Dibert's dream. *Courtesy of Joe and Michelle McAndrew.*

felt when they came upon the dead deer and the child's shoe, exactly as they had been in Jacob's dream. With trepidation, they approached the fallen tree to find the young Cox boys, huddled together but frozen to death. It was estimated that the boys died four days earlier, the day before Jacob first had the dream. Today, one can visit a monument telling the strange and tragic story in the spot the boys were found.

Examined together, these tales provide an interesting overview of Derry's reputation and alleged powers. While cursing three men who mocked her to hang may seem like an overreaction, the second tale involving Cassidy and his friend John Updyke makes Derry's supernatural punishment seem more appropriate. Old Moll's apprentice directly delivers justice that the courts could not provide. In the third tale, Derry warns Polly Williams of imminent danger. It is not an action that one would expect from an evil witch. In the final tale, the witch is recruited to help save the lost children by the community but fails to deliver the requested aid when it is absolutely necessary. If Old Moll was as sinister as sometimes presented, why did she curse evil men and try to prevent the death of a young woman and some lost children? Was she really only a fortune teller and sometime folk healer rumor turned into a witch? Or was she actually a practitioner of the dark

The monument to the Lost Children of the Alleghenies, near the spot where their bodies were located. It is covered by a protective enclosure to prevent vandalism. *Courtesy of Joe and Michelle McAndrew.*

Another view of the location where the bodies of the Cox children were discovered. *Courtesy of Joe and Michelle McAndrew.*

arts? Perhaps there was something else that made Old Moll an outsider? To answer these questions, or at least to attempt to, we will have to set the legends aside for the moment and attempt to find the real Mary Derry. Our search will have to start within the historical record. But first, it is necessary to understand the context in which the belief in folk magic and witchcraft existed in early Pennsylvania.

FOLK HEALERS AND WITCHES IN PENNSYLVANIA

To really know who Mary Derry was, or was at least believed to have been, it is important to understand the beliefs regarding witchcraft that were prevalent in early Pennsylvania. Old Moll existed within a much larger supernatural tradition where witches were thought to be far more common than our modern minds might imagine. They were part of a belief system involving what we would now call folk magic and folk religion. The system encompassed aspects of healing, herbalism, divination, protection and prayer, among other things. It is a tradition that predates the time when there were hard lines between religion, magic and science and was practiced unofficially by common people—hence the term *folk*. Though some aspects of much older pagan traditions were assimilated, these beliefs were situated firmly in the Christian framework by that time, and as we will see, religion played an intricate part in many of the healing and magic practices. Healing and protection often came by invoking God, Jesus, angels or other biblical figures while completing ritual acts. However, if there is supernatural good, then there is usually also supernatural evil. Witches were part of the same belief system, but they drew their power from the devil instead.

Before the advent of modern medicine, most communities in both Europe and early America had individuals who were skilled at these magical/ religious practices and offered healing services. These practitioners existed outside of what we would consider academic or professional medicine. In addition to helping with physical ailments, they also provided forms of protection from evil spirits, created good luck charms, found lost people and animals, looked into the future, protected against thieves and identified witches. Often they were female, but not exclusively, and in Pennsylvania, their numbers were almost equally split between women and men. Publicly, however, a woman was still more likely to be labeled a witch for practicing these folk traditions.

While all cultures have some form of the folk magic practitioner described above, the most documented in the Keystone State is that of the Pennsylvania Germans (or Pennsylvania Dutch, as they are often called). Since Mary Derry was of German descent, she likely would have practiced a variation of the tradition, so it can provide us with some context to her purported magical abilities. Germans came to Pennsylvania early (the late 1600s) and became an indispensable part of the economy and culture of the state. William Penn's policy of religious tolerance drew many members of German religious sects who sought a home free of persecution. Other mainstream Protestant and Catholic Germans came for economic opportunity. They all brought with them traditions of magic and witchcraft.

The Pennsylvania German practice of folk magic has two sides. The good side is known as Braucherei, which is usually translated as "trying" or "using." Braucherei encompasses all of the healing, protective and helpful elements of folk magic. In eastern and central Pennsylvania, this practice is referred to as powwow (not to be confused with the Native American term). The origins of the use of this word are not entirely clear. Opposite of Braucherei is the dark side of folk magic, known as Hexerei. This is the practice of witchcraft and hexes, using magic to cause harm, illness or even death. Although these simple definitions may seem rather clear, in reality, the line between folk healer and witch often became blurred, especially to those looking in on the practice from the outside.

Among the Pennsylvania Germans themselves, there were, and continue to be, more than two different types of practitioners of the folk magic. It is important to note that anyone could participate and use the charms, incantations and rituals; however, some individuals were more adept than others. Often these special individuals would pass the tradition down through their family so that there was a practitioner in each generation. When possible, a family member of the opposite sex was trained, but if none was available, any family member who showed promise would do.

Eminent folklorist and expert on the Pennsylvania German culture Don Yoder identified four different levels of practice. The first was the charmer. A charmer was essentially a dabbler who used simple powwow techniques for occasional healing and protection. They would be indistinguishable

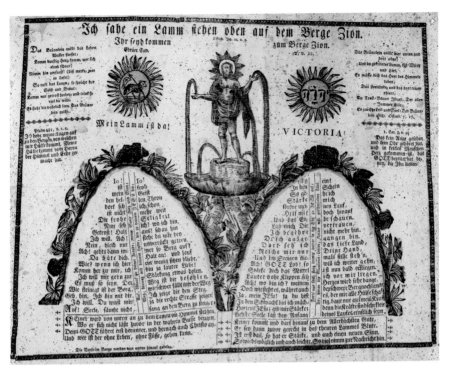

An example of Pennsylvania German Fraktur script depicting a verse from the Book of Revelation. *Courtesy of the Library of Congress, Prints and Photographs Division.*

from anyone else and would encompass the vast majority of those familiar with the traditions.

The second type of practitioner was the powwower or braucher. The powwower possessed a greater understanding of the practice and developed a reputation for his or her ability. The powwower might have been a semiprofessional in the sense that aid did not require a fee, but he or she might accept payment or gifts if offered. (In the twentieth century, a fee was sometimes required depending on the individual.) The powwower might not have served the general community at all but rather family and friends only. Powwowers invoked God and religious figures and offered all of the helpful and healing services described above. Though occasionally viewed with some suspicion, powwowers generally were an accepted part of the community and provided useful services. It is important to note here that the term *powwower* was likely not used in western Pennsylvania during Moll Derry's time, though these healers certainly existed. Among those of English descent, these types of folk healers were known as the cunning folk. The methods of the cunning folk were very similar, and in some ways nearly identical to those of the powwow practitioners, so the core elements of the folk magic would have been mutually understandable between those of German and English heritage.

The third type of practitioner is perhaps the most difficult to define. The hex doctor walked the line between powwower and witch. Hex doctors were often professional or full-time practitioners who accepted various forms of payment. They were highly skilled in Braucherei, divination, reversing hexes and identifying witches. However, some hex doctors understood witchcraft well and were occasionally asked to place hexes of their own. Like powwower, the term *hex doctor* was not used in the western part of the state during Derry's time, although the term *witch master* was common. A witch master, like a hex doctor, had the power to directly challenge a witch. In many of the tales, Old Moll often acted as more of a powwower or hex doctor than an evil witch.

The final type is, of course, the malevolent witch. Witches used folk magic to cause harm to individuals and the community, extract revenge and commit supernatural crimes. Witches drew their power not from God, but from a pact with the devil, which cost them their souls. Richard Shaner recorded several of the alleged methods for making the pact while compiling his research in the mid-twentieth century.

One cruel method required the aspiring witch to boil a black cat alive in a kettle. When the flesh separated, a ladle was used to collect the bones. They were then taken to a stream and tossed in. One bone rose to the surface of the water and floated against the current. The witch then retrieved the bone and gained his or her power. In some accounts, a toad could be substituted for a cat.

Another method required the would-be witch to take a piece of coal and draw a circle on the kitchen floor. The person then stepped inside the circle and put a hand outside. The devil would then appear and mark the supplicant's palm, granting him or her the powers of a witch.

A third method required the person to get a manure hook and then stand on top of a manure pile in a barnyard. The hook had to be swung around the head three times while denying Christ three times. After the denier finished, he or she would be a witch, at the cost of the soul.

With such descriptions, one would think there would be a clear distinction between the folk healer and the witch, but for many, there was only a fine line separating them. Just as it is today, for many people, dabbling in any ritual healing or folk magic was seen as interaction with

A witch embracing the devil as depicted in Ulrich Molitor's *Of Fiends and Witches* from 1489. *Public domain.*

unnatural (and unholy) forces. For others, it was a matter of perspective. If someone had a string of bad luck, they might easily come to believe that a local folk healer, who was already believed to possess supernatural gifts, may have a hidden dark side. Powwowers, hex doctors and witch masters all used techniques to combat witches that essentially reversed a witch's curse. So in some sense, they were also causing curses or supernatural harm, although in a defensive manner. Theoretically, it was possible for anyone to misuse the folk magic system. In such cases, these academic categories of practitioners do not completely reflect the vague complexities of their occult worldview.

The one question that I have not addressed so far is why people believed (and still believe) in the power of folk magic. One obvious and often repeated explanation is that folk magic provided an explanation for otherwise unexplainable happenings. This is especially true in the prescientific world, where other explanations were unknown. The death of otherwise healthy cattle due to an invisible disease might not necessarily be apparent to a farmer. If one did not know about germs and microbes, the sudden death of a healthy cow might seem baffling. However, the unusual old woman who lives on the neighboring farm, with whom he had a recent dispute, might seem more of a culprit. After all, the animal died for some reason. Maybe there were already rumors about the woman using folk magic, and the animal died shortly after the last argument with the woman. To prevent further harm and to stop the woman, the farmer might turn to folk magic himself.

This explanation was certainly true in the premodern world, but it does not explain why the belief in magic and witchcraft has persisted. Another reason that folk magic has endured for so long is that it provides some sense of control over life and the immediate future. Practitioners have traditionally come from the lower classes and bottom half of the middle class. These classes have had less economic and political power and have been subject to the decisions of the upper classes. Throughout most of history, farmers and those who work in agriculture have also been susceptible to the forces of nature. There were (and are) many outside factors that can lead to extreme hardship or death for poor agricultural families. Practicing folk magic (usually the "white" or healing/ protection magic) gave them a chance, and some hope, against these forces that they could not control.

Another reason why the belief in folk magic and other invisible supernatural forces persists even now is the fact that the supernatural allows for a greater meaning to life, whether tied to a religion or just a sense that there is something beyond the physical world. Science, for all its benefits, tells us only how things work. It imparts no real meaning and no sense of purpose. But human beings are not machines, so we seek meaning in the world. Most humans do not desire a cold, mechanical world but rather a world enchanted with purpose. For many, this is found in the belief in folk magic, religion or other supernatural systems. If folk magic works, then that means a greater force exists and it can be interacted with. And if witches are real (in the traditional sense, not modern Neopaganism), that means there is supernatural evil. However, supernatural evil cannot exist without supernatural good, so even though witches are threatening, their very existence confirms the belief that God and forces of supernatural good can be turned to for help.

HOW FOLK MAGIC WORKS

So by now you may be wondering exactly how folk magic and witchcraft actually work, or at least were believed to have worked. As we will soon see, the performance and mechanics of these magical-religious rites may seem bizarre to the modern observer. However, folk magic has its own internal logic and rules. It is guided by two interdependent ideas: contagion and transference. Disease, bad luck and misfortunes are caused by evil and are contagious in the sense that they can be given to or caught by a person, either unintentionally through daily activity and encounters or deliberately because of another person or entity. That may seem to be a bleak view of the world, but there is hope because these evil forces can also be ritually transferred or warded off with the proper preparation. This process is facilitated through the use of ritualized objects that represent individuals and aspects of their person. Folk magic of this type is known academically as sympathetic magic. (Voodoo dolls are probably the most well-known application of sympathetic magic, though they are not part of the Pennsylvania German tradition.) This system, in the prescientific world, provided explanations when bad things happened and hope that problems could be corrected. It also provided a sense of control in a world where most people were at the mercy of powerful elites and of nature itself. Until the twentieth century, rural agricultural life was the norm for most people. Those trying to scratch out a living off the land were especially susceptible to the changes in nature, and agricultural themes are reflected heavily in the folk magic of the Americas and Europe.

To perform folk magic, a folk healer (or a witch, presumably) would use verbal components, actions and physical objects. Spoken prayers, incantations and charms were used regularly, although witches would not use Christian prayers, of course. These would often be accompanied by hand gestures, laying on of hands or the sweeping of hands through the air over parts of the body, especially with healing rituals. For folk healers, verbal prayers and charms were often repeated three times, in imitation of the Holy Trinity. A good example of this is a charm that was commonly used to stop bleeding. The folk healer would breathe on a person's wound and then say the Lord's Prayer, stopping at the word *Earth*. After the healer did this tree times, the bleeding would cease. Another example is a remedy to help heal burns. It combines a spoken charm and physical actions. First, the healer says, "Blow, I blow on thee!" and then breathes three times quickly on the wound with the same breath. Immediately after, the healer makes the sign of the Cross three times over the wound.

Written charms were also common and could be prepared by a folk healer for use when they were not available. Some would be folded up and could be carried in one's pocket or bag. Others would be posted in homes and barns. Some were even fed to farm animals to cure them from illness or to protect from hexes. These paper amulets were very popular, not just in America but in Europe as well, and were relatively inexpensive. For example, if one was suffering from a fever, the following charm was to be written on white paper and sewn to a piece of linen, then hung around the neck until the fever broke:

AbaxaCatabaxa
AbaxaCatabax
AbaxaCataba
AbaxaCatab
AbaxaCata
AbaxaCat
AbaxaCa
AbaxaC
Abaxa
Abax
Aba
Ab
A

Other variations use the word *AbraCadabra* (Yes—it is a real magic word!)

Ritualized objects and materials were also frequently used in conjunction with verbal and written charms or on their own. Many of these objects were mundane but took on a greater meaning in the ritual. Pennies, eggs, potatoes, thread, ropes, knives, scissors, stones, burning coals, animal parts and horse collars were just some of the objects that were incorporated into rituals. Traditional religious objects such as Bibles and holy water were frequently used as well. Even saliva and other bodily fluids played a role in some rituals. In the Gospel of John, Jesus used his saliva to cure a blind man, so folk healers mimicked the process. In his superb study *Powwowing among the Pennsylvania Dutch*, David Kriebel points out that bodily secretions were viewed as a magical agent of transmission that could heal or cause harm, depending on the circumstance. A common example of the use of a ritualized object was the practice of using a potato to remove warts. There are several variations to the practice, but it was usually something like the following. A potato was sliced in half and then rubbed on the wart three times. This may or may not have been accompanied by a spoken charm. Then the potato was taken outside and buried (preferably six feet underground). As the potato decayed, the wart vanished. Alternatively, the potato could be taken and tossed into running water or even fed to pigs for the same effect. By burying the potato, the practitioner was symbolically destroying the evil that caused it, as if burying a corpse. Running water has long been thought to trap evil or form a barrier to it in European folklore, and transferring the evil to the pigs mimics the Gospel passage where Jesus drives the demons from a possessed man and they are forced to inhabit swine.

Another example of a ritualized object is what one could jokingly call a magic fire extinguisher. If one needed to extinguish a fire without water, a plate with a SATOR square inscribed on both sides would work. The plate would simply need to be tossed into the fire to put it out. A SATOR square is a Latin palindrome that has a long history of use in European occult traditions. It dates to the time of the Romans, but its original meaning is still debated among scholars. It looks like this:

$$
\begin{array}{l}
\text{S A T O R} \\
\text{A R E P O} \\
\text{T E N E T} \\
\text{O P E R A} \\
\text{R O T A S}
\end{array}
$$

Objects like this were very common. Just a few years ago, one was discovered near a fireplace in Pittsburgh's old Deutschtown neighborhood.

We have already alluded to the uses of these verbal and written charms, prayers, actions and objects, but now we can look at them in greater detail, especially with regards to witchcraft. For folk healers/powwowers and hex doctors/witch masters, much of their time was spent on providing healing and protection from both natural and supernatural dangers. They also frequently helped find lost animals, people and property; identify and trap thieves; mend objects; charm rifles; conjure angels; and, of course, practice divination of future events. Witches, on the other hand, would use these methods to cause illness and hardships; harass neighbors; cause crop failure and sickness in animals; steal milk and other possessions; change shape into cats, wolves or other animals; and even conjure demons and evil spirits.

Many of the charms used by both folk healers and witches were passed by word of mouth in Moll Derry's time. Some families recorded them in recipe books along with more mundane home remedies and recipes for food and drink. There would be variations in the specifics of charms because of this, but a remarkable consistency seems to have been retained nonetheless. In 1820, German Catholic immigrant John George Hohman, who was himself a powwower, broke the tradition of keeping the charms private when he published *Der Lange Verborgene Freund*, or *The Long Lost Friend*, in Reading, Pennsylvania. The book was a collection of charms that he thought should be shared with his fellow man to alleviate their suffering. In what was either an earnest attempt to help or a clever marketing ploy, the book itself served as a talisman of sorts, promising to protect its bearer from harm. It says:

> *Whoever carries this book with him, is safe from all his enemies, visible or invisible; and whoever has this book with him cannot die without the holy corpse of Jesus Christ, nor drowned in any water, nor burn up in any fire, nor can any unjust sentence be passed upon him. So help me.* +++

It quickly became popular among powwowers and allowed people dabbling in folk magic greater access to once-hidden remedies. While Derry almost certainly never saw the book, it does provide insight into the types of charms circulating among Pennsylvania's German population while she was alive. While a witch would not have much of a use for the book because it contained benevolent magic, it does provide some examples of how one can protect oneself from witchcraft and supernatural assault.

Above: A knife and a Bible, two objects frequently used in powwow rituals and charms. *Courtesy of Robert Phoenix.*

Right: The title page of the original 1820 German-language edition of *The Long Lost Friend*. *Author's collection.*

Der lange

Verborgene Freund,

ober:

Getreuer und Chriftlicher

Unterricht für jedermann,

enthaltend:

Wunderbare und probmäßige

Mittel und Künste,

Sowohl für die Menschen als das Vieh.

Mit vielen Zeugen bewiefen in diefem Buch, und wovon das Mehrfte noch wenig bekannt ift, und zum allererften Mal in America im Druck erfcheint.

———

Herausgegeben
von
Sohann Georg Hohman,
Nahe bey Reading, in Elfaß Taunfchip, Berks Caunty, Pennfylvanien.

Reading:
Gedruckt für den Verfaßer.
1820.

One of the most often used charms against supernatural evil would be written on a piece of paper and carried on one's person at all times. Hohman described the charm as "Against Evil Spirits and All Manner of Witchcraft." It looked like this:

I.

N. I. R.

I.

SANCTUS SPIRITUS.

I.

N. I. R.

I.

All this be guarded here in time, and there in eternity. Amen.

Hohman states that the letters signify "God bless me here in time, and there eternally." To protect cattle from witchcraft, Hohman prescribes writing a SATOR square (see page 35) on a piece of paper and adding it to their feed. Once an animal swallows the charm, it will be safe from the assault of a witch. He also included other spoken charms that protected against a variety of evils that might befall a person, including witchcraft. One example was titled "To Prevent Being Cheated, Charmed or Bewitched, and to Be at All Times Blessed." It reads:

Like unto the cup and the wine, and the holy supper, which our dear Lord Jesus Christ gave unto his disciples on Maunday [sic] Thursday, may the Lord Jesus guard me in daytime, and at night, that no dog may bite me, no wild beast tear me to pieces, no tree fall on me, no water rise against me, no fire-arms injure me, no weapons, no steel, no iron, cut me, no fire burn me, no false sentence fall upon me, no false tongue injure me, no rogue enrage me, and that no fiends, no witchcraft and enchantment can harm me. Amen.

This charm is interesting in the fact that it covers almost everything that your average person in the early 1800s might be afraid of. It demonstrates that the fear of witchcraft was as real as the fear of being mauled by an animal or murdered. For many, witchcraft was just another part of the world that they lived in.

Hohman was by no means the only source of preventative anti-witchcraft charms. Many others have survived in various forms throughout Pennsylvania and in the Appalachians. One common charm could be placed on the headboard of a person's bed or over the front door or barn door:

> *Trotter head, I forbid thee my house and premises; I forbid thee my horse and cow stable; I forbid thee my bedstead, that thou mayest not breathe upon me; breathe into some other house, until thou hast ascended every hill, until thou hast counted every fencepost, and until thou hast crossed every water. And thus dear day may come again into my house, in the name of God the Father, the Son, and the Holy Ghost. Amen.*

If you are wondering, the term *trotter head*, or *trottenkopf* in German, originates in southern Germany and is a Pennsylvania Dutch variation of a word meaning "malevolent spirits" or "goblins." This charm is widespread geographically with some slight variations, but they all demand that the evil goblin or spirit perform the seemingly impossible task of climbing up every hill in the world, crossing every body of water and counting every fence post before it can inflict any harm. Traditional lore holds that goblins were proud creatures who would not turn down a challenge to complete a task, even an impossible one, and they would not return until it was completed. In addition to written paper charms and spoken incantations, other methods could be used to deter witches, especially from entering barns. Many old barns had five-pointed stars (pentagrams) carved on the inside somewhere over the door. These were called *hexafoos*, or the "witch's foot." Though today pentagrams are often associated with Satanism, the Pennsylvania Germans believed that this symbol could prevent a witch from entering. Other options included mixing cow and hog blood and sprinkling it above every doorframe and window or placing a toad's foot or a goose's foot within a hexafoo on or above a door. If one preferred a method involving less butchering of animals, hanging a horseshoe above the door would also help to ward off malevolent supernatural forces. It was also believed that placing a broomstick across a doorway would prevent a witch from entering because it was thought that a witch would not step over a broomstick. There was even a method to test if you suspected that a person who entered your house was a witch. If you placed the end of a broom in the oven, a witch would become more and more uncomfortable as it heated up and would be forced to leave. If your guest was unaffected, you were safe. (For additional examples of charms and folk magic, see the appendix.)

A protection charm carved into a fence post. *Courtesy of Robert Phoenix.*

Often the charms and forms of protection that were used against witchcraft were not enough to stop a hex or curse from occurring. It was believed that some witches were very powerful or may have had direct help from the devil or evil spirits. In cases such as this, the afflicted might turn to the hex doctor/witch master for help. They were more adept at fighting witches directly and had methods for reversing the magical assault. However, before we examine their practices, we first have to look at the folk magic of the witches themselves.

Witches existed in the same system of folk magic but drew their power from evil sources. As a result, most of their magic was focused on causing harm to individuals and their livelihoods. When a witch placed a hex on a person or animal, the recipient might suffer anything from mild harassment to fatal illness. Crop failure was often attributed to the work of a witch. A hex ring was a circular area of ground where no vegetation could grow. It was assumed that some form of magic circle was put in place to cause the defoliation. (In some ways, it is similar to the faerie ring tradition of Celtic Europe.) Often the crop failure was on a larger scale and could spell financial ruin. Even though there are plenty of natural reasons why a crop might not yield what was expected, assigning the problem to a witch gave an unlucky farmer someone to blame.

Witches could also wreak havoc with food. Making butter was a regular occurrence on early Pennsylvania farms. Most of the time there were no problems, but whenever it proved impossible to properly churn butter, a witch might be suspected. Witches could also become the prime suspect if a cow failed to produce milk. In fact, the stealing of milk was one of the occurrences most commonly associated with witches. The witch need only get a hair from the cow (or, in some cases, simply name it) or have something that ritually represents the animal, wrap it in a towel with a pin and place it over a chair or doorknob. Then the witch could place a bucket underneath and "milk" the towel like it was a cow. The milk would mysteriously drip out into the bucket. Many miles away, the unsuspecting farmer's cow went dry and had no milk for the farmer's family. Witches were also thought to curse milk so it would turn bloody and unusable. To stop this from occurring again, the milk had to be heated and stirred in an X pattern. Witches could also stop bread from rising and even hex cooking pots. Richard Shaner, in his 1973 pamphlet *Hexerei*, reported, "When three small balls with a silvery luster are found in the family dinner pot, that family has been bewitched. To break the spell take the silver balls and shoot them into a white oak tree." It was believed that witches could even stop cider from turning to vinegar. Essentially, any part of the food-making process could be disrupted by a hex. On a large enough scale, this could conceivably cause tremendous difficulty for farmers.

Cattle and other farm animals were also considered to be frequent targets of witches. Any time an animal fell ill, failed to produce milk or suffered from a disease, there was a chance that a farmer might believe that he and his livestock were hexed. One common occurrence that was attributed to witches but now has a rather mundane explanation was the discovery of giant balls of hair in the stomachs of cattle. Farmers often called these witch balls, and they believed that witches would "shoot" them into the stomachs of animals. Given that farmers were more likely to slaughter cows that did not produce enough milk, the discovery of a witch ball could confirm fears that witchcraft had been afflicting the cattle all along. Of course, we now know that some animals will lick or accidentally eat their own fur, which accumulates in their stomachs, but that explanation did not exist at the time. Cattle, in particular, do not vomit, so they cannot expel the hair balls once they form. Possession of a witch ball, recovered from a dead animal, was believed to grant the bearer the power to hex others, so if discovered, they were often burned.

Horses were frequent targets of witchcraft. When farmers would come to the stable in the morning and discover that their horses were "lathered up" and irritated, it was thought that a witch had been riding them all night. The exhausted animals would be of no use to the farmer the next day. In severe instances, it was thought that a witch could cause a horse or other animal to be possessed by an evil spirit. In these cases, hex doctors/witch masters may not even be able to help. The animal would become uncontrollable, and the farmer would be forced to shoot it with a silver bullet.

The belief that one was hexed could be amplified if the animals and crops on neighbors' farms were doing well while one's own were suffering. Any string of bad luck could be attributed to a hex. In difficult times, it was perhaps more comforting to have an explanation in the local witch rather than none at all. When witches were blamed for personal afflictions and ailments, the system of folk magic could suddenly be taken very seriously.

It was commonly believed that a witch could inflict physical harm on individuals in a variety of manners. A long wasting illness was often attributed to supernatural assault. Witches had the ability to block the body from receiving nourishment from food, resulting in a long, drawn-out suffering. Seizures, fits, choking and the sensation of being stabbed and poked with needles or burning were all trademarks of a witch's hex. It was sometimes believed that the witch was present but invisible, inflicting this harm directly on his/her victim. Other times it could be carried out at a distance. A witch could turn invisible by performing a rather disturbing ritual. The witch had to take the ear of a black cat, boil it in the milk of a black cow and then make a thumb covering of it and wear it. Witches could also supposedly see in the dark by wiping the blood of a bat across their eyes.

Even in one's own bedroom, you were not safe from witches. A hexed person might discover the feathers in a pillow woven into a wreath. These witch wreaths were used to place a hex on unsuspecting victims who might never think to check their own pillows as the source. To break the hex, it had to be undone or ritually disposed of. Many reports exist of people being "ridden" by witches at night. Victims might wake to the horrific sight and pressure of the witch on top of them. Unable to move, they were forced to endure the assault until the witch vanished and they could move again. If a prayer or protective charm was said, even if it was not out loud, it might cause the witch to leave. Some even believed that they were ridden like a horse (and possibly transformed into one) into the countryside.

While today this phenomenon has been studied and (at least partially) explained by sleep paralysis or "Old Hag" syndrome, at the time it was not understood. When sleep paralysis occurs, the body is in a hypnagogic or twilight state between being awake and asleep. Vivid dreams can seem real, and the brain has not told the body to start moving yet, so to the semiconscious mind it can feel like being paralyzed. This state does not usually last very long—often less than a minute—but it can be frightening. The pressure on the chest is the weight of one's own body, which is not felt while awake. Between the pressure and the dream/nightmare-induced vision of the witch or hag, it is completely understandable why this experience would be viewed as a supernatural assault in the past.

If all of these afflictions and hexes were not enough, witches were also believed to have familiars, which were animals or spirits in the form of animals who helped witches carry out their dark magic. (Recall the belief that Moll Derry controlled rattlesnakes.) These would occasionally appear in witch tales around the state, and the sightings of strange animals often were viewed as an indication that a witch was targeting a family or individual. More frequently, the witches would transform into animals such as black cats and wolves to harass or cause physical harm to neighbors and animals. Wolves were a real threat to livestock into the mid-1800s in parts of Pennsylvania, so like other threats, they were sometimes assigned a supernatural cause in the form of a shape-shifting witch or werewolf. (To read more about the authentic werewolf legends of Pennsylvania, see the book *Supernatural Lore of Pennsylvania: Ghosts, Monsters and Miracles.*) Familiars and shape-shifting witches were blamed when an unfamiliar animal appeared and exhibited unusual behavior. If a farmer could injure the animal, it would often help reveal the witch. For example, if a farmer shot a wolf that was prowling around the barn and then saw a woman who lived nearby with her arm in a sling the next morning, he might believe that she was the witch.

So with all of the formidable afflictions that a witch might set upon his/her enemy, hex doctors and witch masters needed equally powerful folk magic to break the hexes. Charms existed specifically to drive out witches, and they were often used in conjunction with pins, knives, silver objects, boiling or running water, herbs and even bodily fluids. For any given hex or curse there might be several possible ways to counteract it.

For example, if a witch prevented your butter from churning, a hex doctor might suggest putting a red-hot horseshoe into the churn to break the spell. Another option would be to take hazel switches and lash the churn. The witch would feel the lashing and release his or her hold on the churn. Finally, there is the option of shooting the churn with a silver bullet. While this would damage your churn, it would also kill the witch who had hexed it. A silver bullet fired at an inanimate object to break a hex or kill a witch is called a Hexeschuss. In the next chapter, there is an example from Warren County of one of the common witch-killing methods involving a Hexeschuss. Witches were always considered highly susceptible to silver.

Silver bullets were not the only way to kill a witch. If your cow had been hexed (and presumably died as a result), you could take its heart or a piece of its heart, fry it in butter and prepare it as if it were a meal. Then you would pierce it with three nails taken from a coffin that held a corpse. Wherever the witch was, he/she would feel his/her heart pierced and would die. The witch's hexes would be broken. An alternative that would not involve the death of the witch but that would still end the hex would be to boil the heart, perhaps poking it occasionally with pins. The witch would feel the tremendous pain and end the hex and might even arrive at the victim's door and beg them to stop.

One method for stopping and killing a witch we saw demonstrated in an earlier chapter by Moll Derry's apprentice. It was believed to have worked on evil and guilty people as well, which is why it was used on John Updyke. If the likeness of the witch was drawn on a piece of wood, a nail could be driven in a little each day for nine days, causing pain for the witch and eventual death. This particular method was also very common in the African American Hoodoo/Conjure tradition.

Most techniques used against witches were not lethal though. Your average person did not want to kill out of revenge, only end the torment. If cows produced bloody milk, a farmer might boil the liquid or stab and slash it with a knife to inflict pain on the witch so the hex was ended. If someone was suffering from a witch-induced illness, he or she might create a witch bottle. A witch bottle provided a way to reverse a curse and cause the witch to suffer instead. If one was suffering from a hex that affected the digestive system, one might fill a bottle with urine and three or seven pins to represent the pain. It would then be corked or sealed and buried or locked away in an airtight box. Until the bottle was reopened, the witch would suffer from the pain of the affliction and, in some cases, beg the formerly hexed person to open the bottle. Usually, the witch would not harass that person again.

Another nonlethal way to break a hex involved running water. The idea that evil may have difficulty crossing moving water has appeared at various times in European folklore. Americans who have researched vampire legends may be familiar with this as a way to evade the undead. The idea also existed in German lore about witches. It was thought that the witch, or at least her hex, could not travel across a stream or river. Hex doctors and witch masters might advise taking a hexed person across a stream to break the curse, and crossing two streams would be even better. You could never be too careful with witches after all.

These are just a few examples of methods used to fight witchcraft in the Pennsylvania German tradition. Many variations of these exist, and sometimes the specifics of the ritual depend on individual circumstance. In the next chapter, we will examine some examples of hexes and the methods used to combat them as they occurred in local cases of witchcraft. Before we proceed, there is still one area of folk magic usable by healers or witches that is central to the legend of Moll Derry. Divination, or the practice of seeing the future or seeking knowledge of the unknown through supernatural methods, has existed in many forms since ancient times. One of the reasons that folk healers and hex doctors/witch masters were often sought out was to find lost items, treasure, sources of water and minerals—and to see into the future. There were a variety of charms, methods and ritualized objects that would be used to carry out the divination.

One was the dowsing rod or wand. In the proper hands, such a rod, usually *Y* shaped, could point the way to lost treasure, mineral deposits and water sources (which is why it is sometimes known as water witching). Often the branches of specific trees had to be used. *The Long Lost Friend* included two sets of instructions for making a dowsing rod:

> *To Make a Wand for Searching for Iron, Ore or Water*
>
> *On the first night of Christmas, between 11 and 12 o'clock, break off from any tree a young twig of one year's growth, in the three highest names (Father, Son and Holy Ghost), at the same time facing toward sunrise. Whenever you apply this wand in searching for anything apply it three times. The twig must be forked, and each end of the fork must be held in one hand, so that the third and thickest part of it stands up, but do not hold it too tight. Strike the ground with the thickest end, and that which you desire will appear immediately, if there is any in the ground where you strike. The words to be spoken when the wand is thus applied are as follows:*
>
> > *Archangel Gabriel, I conjure thee in the name of God, the Almighty, to tell me, is there any water here or not? Do tell me! +++*
>
> *If you are searching for Iron or Ore, you have to say the same, only mention the name of what you are searching for.*

And:

> *Words to Be Spoken While Making Divinatory Wands.*
>
> *In making divinatory wands, they must be broke as before directed, and while breaking and before using them, the following words must be spoken:*
>
> > *Divining rod, do thou keep that power,*
> > *Which God gave unto thee at the very first hour.*

A dowsing rod created by contemporary powwow practitioner Robert Phoenix. *Courtesy of Robert Phoenix.*

Other methods of divination could see the future and find missing people and animals. One device, often associated with witches, that could be used for this purpose was an Erdspiegel, or "earth mirror." The Erdspiegel was a special mirror placed in the bottom of a sack or bag (often black) that was sometimes filled with some soil or dirt. By looking into the bag, the witch or practitioner could see visions in the mirror, much like a crystal ball. These were believed to be especially powerful and effective.

Other folk magic practitioners used tasseography, or reading coffee grounds or tea leaves after one has consumed the beverage. The positions of the remaining grounds or tea leaves in the cup were thought to reveal clues about the future of the one who drank it. While this practice and others, like palmistry (palm reading), were not unique to the Pennsylvania Germans, there were those who incorporated elements of other traditions in their work. Later we will see that Moll Derry was known for practicing tasseography. All of these methods of divination appear in the following chapters.

OTHER CASES OF
WITCHCRAFT AND MAGIC
IN WESTERN PENNSYLVANIA

As mentioned previously, Moll Derry was not the only witch in the Keystone State. Pennsylvania is home to hundreds of alleged instances of witchcraft, dating from the late 1600s well into the twentieth century. The belief in folk healing, magic and witchcraft has always been strong, lurking under the veneer of rational modern civilization. Pennsylvania may have been home to Enlightenment-era ideas of liberty, heavy industry and advances in technology and medicine, but it was also home to many different religious and ethnic groups with their own supernatural beliefs. Witches, it seems, were with the state from the very beginning. As a Quaker leader and founder of the Pennsylvania colony, William Penn himself once presided over a witch trial in the settlement's earliest days. The verdict of the trial set the precedent for the way witchcraft would be handled in Pennsylvania from that time forward.

In February 1684, Margaret Mattson and Yethro Hendrickson found themselves in the unfortunate position of being the first people officially brought to trial for witchcraft in the young colony. Both women were of Swedish descent. Their families had been part of the former colony of New Sweden along the Delaware River. That colony passed to the British and was part of the area granted to William Penn in 1681 by the king. Penn, known for his tolerant policies, especially in regards to religion, had allowed the remaining Swedish colonists to stay. Both of the accused women spoke little English, and the surviving testimony includes no statements from Hendrickson.

Several accusers came forward with testimony, which was shaky at best. A man named Henry Drystreet claimed that he had been told twenty years earlier that Mattson was a witch and that she had cursed the cattle of a local farmer. Charles Ashcom insisted that Mattson had threatened her own daughter in spectral form, appearing at the foot of her bed with a knife. Another local woman, Annakey Coolin, believed that her family's cattle were the victims of Mattson's spells. In an attempt to draw out the witch using counter-magic, her husband boiled the heart of one of the sickened calves. During this process, a haggard and agitated Margaret Mattson allegedly came to the door, demanding to know what they were doing. They explained their motives, to which Mattson retorted that they should have boiled the bones instead. The Coolins took this as an indication of Mattson's guilt. She denied all of the charges, of course.

For a long time, an apocryphal story has circulated about a humorous exchange at the trial. Supposedly, William Penn himself asked Mattson if she had ever flown through the air on a broomstick. Because of the language barrier, she misunderstood the question and answered yes. Penn wittily replied that there was no law against riding through the air on a broomstick.

When the testimony concluded, Penn gave the jury very specific instructions. They quickly rendered an unusual verdict. Mattson was guilty of "having the common fame of being a witch, but not guilty in the manner and form she stands indicted." Her punishment was a fine of fifty pounds and sixth months of guaranteed good behavior under her husband's supervision (essentially house arrest).

Though the verdict may seem bizarre to us today, it was actually a wise one. Penn allowed a minor punishment that appeased the accusers. It was clear that Mattson was not liked and was involved in problems in the community (whether they were her fault or not). Quakers put little stock in tales of witches, believing that humanity was evil enough already. However, by not actually convicting her of witchcraft, he established a precedent

Engraving of William Penn. *Courtesy of the Library of Congress, Prints and Photographs Division.*

that would be followed in Pennsylvania in the future. The courts of Penn's Woods would not prosecute witchcraft, so believers had to turn elsewhere for help against the perceived supernatural threat. Folk healers, cunning folk, practitioners of powwow, hex doctors, witch masters and the like were the only option that remained to battle witches and their hexes.

The use of folk magic by the Pennsylvania Germans is especially well documented. There are probably several reasons why, including the fact that in the early years, the Germans were different culturally and their "unusual" traditions drew commentary from English and Scots-Irish observers. The English were more likely to make a hard distinction between mysticism and the supernatural on one hand and the rational and scientific world on the other. English folk healing and folk magic traditions were there, but they were generally looked on as backward by the 1800s, at least publicly. In the German cultural tradition, mysticism and rationalism were not always assumed to be in opposition. As a result, the Pennsylvania Germans were generally more likely to openly practice folk healing and folk magic and, in the process, create more usable sources for modern-day researchers. The strong presence of academic folklore programs in the state also created an extensive body of research on Pennsylvania German life.

Because of these conditions, we have been able to see just how extensive such practices were, not only in Pennsylvania Dutch country but beyond as well. Tales of magical healings, fateful predictions and witch's hexes can be found in virtually every county. Western Pennsylvania has its share of these accounts. Of course, some traces of the English cunning folk traditions also survive and mix with German traditions in western Pennsylvania. To get a better sense of the enchanted world in which Moll Derry operated, it will be useful to examine a few of these tales and reports from the nineteenth century.

Reading the numerous county and regional histories that were published between 1870 and 1910, one will realize that many of them contain at least a few paragraphs referencing the extensive belief in supernatural forces in the colonial era and early republic. These histories are unanimous in their dismissal of these ideas, in part to demonstrate the progress that their respective counties had achieved in the Industrial and Progressive eras. In reality, the authors of these volumes were, at best, a single generation removed from the beliefs they described, but in most cases, such beliefs still flourished, just not as publicly as they once had.

In his 1876 book *Notes on the Settlement and Indian Wars of the Western Parts of Virginia and Pennsylvania from 1763 to 1783*, Joseph Doddridge includes a chapter titled "The Witchcraft Delusion." Much of the chapter was later quoted directly in Thomas Cushing's 1889 book *History of Allegheny County, Pennsylvania*. Doddridge stated:

> *The belief in witchcraft was prevalent among the early settlers of the western country. To the witch was ascribed the tremendous power of inflicting strange and incurable diseases, particularly on children, of destroying cattle by shooting them with hair balls, and a great variety of other means of destruction, of inflicting spells and curses on guns and other things, and lastly of changing men into horses, and after bridling and saddling them, riding them in full speed over hill and dale to their frolics and other places of rendezvous. More ample powers of mischief than these cannot well be imagined.*

As we have seen, these are common charges leveled against witches. The belief was certainly widespread enough to warrant a five-and-a-quarter-page chapter in his book, albeit a dismissive one. Doddridge went on to describe male practitioners of folk magic, whom he labeled "wizards":

> *Wizards were men supposed to possess the same mischievous powers as the witches; but these were seldom exercised for bad purposes. The powers of the wizards were exercised almost exclusively for the purpose of counteracting the malevolent influences of the witches of the other sex. I have known several of those witch masters, as they were called, who made a public profession of curing the disease inflicted by the influence of witches, and I have known respectable physicians who had no greater portion of business in the line of their profession, than many of those witch masters had in theirs.*

Doddridge seems to be describing what would be known in eastern and central Pennsylvania as hex doctors. He personally attests to their popularity, claiming that they were just as popular as "respectable physicians." This is not surprising, considering that people he labeled as respectable physicians in the 1800s would likely be considered quacks today or, at the very least, be said to use questionable methods by modern standards. One may very well have received what was perceived as better treatment from a hex doctor or powwower. Of course, Doddridge shows his bias, or perhaps that of the witch masters he knew, by stating that the males practiced only helpful or protective magic whereas women were the primary source of evil magic. While it was far more likely that a woman would be publicly referred to as a witch, there were definitely female folk healers in Pennsylvania, just as there were men who were thought to practice black magic.

In 1882, George Dallas Albert edited *The History of the County of Westmoreland, Pennsylvania*. Several pages were spent discussing the customs and superstitions of the German settlers of the county, which lies directly north of Fayette. He included the following description of the German belief in witchcraft:

> *In that age—we mean the early Westmoreland age—many houses had horseshoes nailed to the lintels of the doors to protect the inmates from the power of witches. Brimstone was burnt to keep them away from the hen-coop, and the breastbone of a chicken put in a little bag and hung around the necks of the children to ward off whooping cough. Horse nails were carried for good luck, and beaux hunted for four-leaved clovers to get their sweethearts to look upon them favorably. A broth made from dried fox lungs was given to patients suffering with consumption, and carrying the rattles of a rattlesnake which had been killed without biting itself would cure the headache and protect from sun-stroke. Old women were even blamed for riding the unbroken colts at night, and more than one person incurred displeasure because his neighbor's rye was worse blasted than his own.*

Aside from the last sentence, Albert's short passage describes traditional folk healing charms and wards against witchcraft rather than actual malevolent magic. Still, it attests to the prevalence of the belief in the power of supernatural forces in daily life. Several lines in the Reverend Joseph H. Bausman's *History of Beaver County, Pennsylvania and Its Centennial Celebration* from 1904 echo the commonality of folk healing and folk magic in western Pennsylvania:

> *A great variety of charms were resorted to for the cure of diseases. They ascribed the infliction of many diseases and calamities to the influence of witches, and believed in the power of wizards, or witch-masters as they were sometimes called, to remove them.*

Though these previously cited writers spoke in generalities about the beliefs regarding healing and the supernatural world, there are many accounts of specific incidents in western Pennsylvania that have survived. One of these was the pseudo witch trial that occurred in 1802 in Allegheny County. Judge B.F. Brewster, who later wrote about the occurrence, lived in Harmar Township on Twelve Mile Island (located in the Allegheny River). One day, a mob of people, dragging a local woman, showed up on his estate.

The woman was frightened, and the judge soon learned why. Her neighbors brought her to the island so that the judge could try her on the charge of practicing witchcraft. Sensing the seriousness of the mob, the judge agreed to try the woman. He believed that they would be unable to produce any evidence and come to their senses once it was discussed. However, his faith in his fellow citizens was misplaced, as individuals came forward with anecdotes that they believed proved the woman's involvement in the dark arts. The tension escalated when a few people in the crowd started asking if she could be executed.

At this point, Brewster took the woman inside his house "under arrest" and told the crowd that he had to consult his legal books. While inside, he had her secretly taken out the back and put on a small boat so she could be sent downriver to Pittsburgh. When the judge finally emerged, he told the impatient crowd that he could not render a verdict because the woman was no longer there. Though several members of the crowd threatened the judge, they eventually dispersed.

Somerset County, which borders Fayette to the east, has been home to many tales of witchcraft and folk magic. The county had a large Pennsylvania German population. In 1892, the *Somerset Herald* ran a lengthy article containing the remembrances of an old-timer named "Uncle Joe"

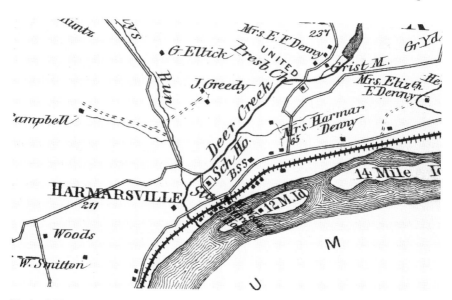

Twelve Mile Island was the home of Judge B.F. Brewster and the site of an impromptu witch trial in 1902. It is depicted here on a map from 1872. *Courtesy of the University Archives and Special Collections at the Gumberg Library, Duquesne University.*

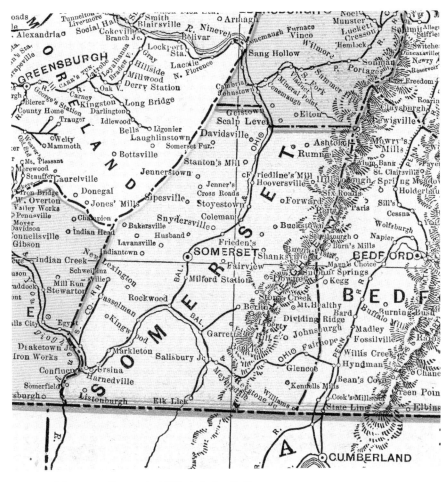

A map of Somerset County in 1890. *Author's collection.*

who described several cases from earlier in that century. One of his accounts, which was sparse on details, described a family being harassed by a witch. Though the form the harassment took was not described, it was substantial enough that the family brought in a "witch doctor" (another term used interchangeably with witch master and hex doctor). The witch master recited charms and then proceeded to bend a needle into a loop until the tip passed through the eye. Early the next morning, the woman who was suspected of being the witch was found doubled over in pain (basically taking the shape of the needle) and lying in a manure pile. She never bothered the family again, and we can assume that the witch doctor unbent the needle, releasing her from the agony it inflicted.

The article also related the story of a man who was being "ridden" by a witch on a regular basis. At night, the witch would appear in his bed and climb on top of him. After assaulting him in his bed, she transported him to a nearby road by some magical means and continued to ride him like a horse. They traveled down roads and through fields until the witch would leave him tied to a post and disappear. In the morning, the man would awaken in his own bed, exhausted. He would try to find the post in the daytime but never could. On his nighttime rides, he even attempted to mark the spot so that he could find his way back, but he was never successful and could never understand how he returned to his bed. This particular tale seems to be a classic case of Old Hag syndrome/sleep paralysis, as discussed in the previous chapter.

One of Joe's other tales involved a house in West Salisbury that was home to four beautiful young women. A local young man decided to pay a visit to the women one day, and when he approached the house, he saw four black cats on the roof. The cats acted strangely, and as he stared, they disappeared right before his eyes. The young man quickly went to the door, and as he was being let in, he found the four young women coming down the steps to meet him. Their hair looked like it had been blowing in the wind, and he had the distinct impression they had been outside. When asked, the women simply said that they had just returned from a walk. The young man felt the same uneasy feeling that he had while looking at the cats and decided not to stay long, fearing the women may have been witches.

Also included was a brief tale of a diabolical pact gone awry (as they usually do). Joe described an unnamed wicked man who had sold his soul to the devil to escape earthly punishments. Every time he was arrested, he called on the devil to get him out of trouble, reminding him of their deal. This happened many times over many years. Finally, the wicked man was arrested on a capital crime that would result in his execution. This time, when he invoked the devil, Satan appeared with a large bag of shoes over his shoulder. The devil explained that these were all the shoes that he had worn out attending to the man's affairs, and now he did not have money to buy more. There would be no help coming this time. Of course, the wicked man was executed, and the devil collected his soul.

Finally, the article contained the story of John Summy's strange encounter on Negro Mountain. When Summy was a young man, he made a trip to visit a young widow and her children who lived on the far side of the mountain. He had heard rumors that she was a witch but dismissed them outright. He found the woman attractive, and she seemed to be attracted to him. Summy stayed a good part of the day, and the woman convinced him to have dinner there as well. As the evening settled in, the woman asked Summy to stay overnight. Summy explained that he could not, and he noticed a sudden change in the woman's mood. He knew she was not happy that he was leaving, and a tinge of fear crept into his mind that the rumors might be true. When Summy began his long walk home, the full moon was already in the sky, and a fresh snowfall reflected its light and illuminated his path. A short distance into his journey, he heard a noise overhead and looked up to see a flock of ducks circling above him. A moment later, they landed on a small mound nearby. Something about the ducks unnerved him, so he picked up a stick and tossed it in their direction. The stick passed through the birds and they vanished. Summy picked up his pace. He knew that if he took a trail through the woods, in two miles he would come to a farmhouse. As he passed through the trees, it became very dark, and he soon began hearing a strange sound. He would later describe it as the wailing of cats. They seemed to be all around him, but he could not see anything. Summy's pace changed to a sprint as he ran full speed to the farmhouse. The owners could tell he was terrified, and they allowed him to stay the night. In the morning, his curiosity got the better of him, and he returned to the path in the woods. He expected to find hundreds of cat tracks in the snow, but the only tracks he found were his own.

In 1883, a Connellsville newspaper reported that the family of farmer Jesse Miller was under supernatural assault in Greenville Township. A series of disturbing events had occurred in his house over the previous months. Objects as heavy as a saddle were being moved around inside the house when no one was there. Miller's wife would exit a room for a minute and return to find folded laundry tossed about the room. The Millers' daughter was thrown from her bed twice by an invisible force. She claimed that she could see the invisible witch and said she was "an old woman with hoary locks, a hairy face, and wearing a thin white cap." The article reported that they were going to hire a local witch doctor to fight the witch, but it seems that there was no follow-up article, so we do not know what ultimately happened.

Farther north in Lawrence County, we are lucky that Esther Black, a professor at Ashland College in Ohio, collected several witch-related accounts in the 1960s. One of the tales she gathered involved an old woman who caused trouble for her neighbors in Big Beaver Township in the mid- and late 1800s. Locals began to notice that every time the old woman was around, bad things would happen: the cows would not produce milk, cream would not churn into butter, fires would not light, bread would not rise and children and animals would misbehave. A cattle buyer from New Castle named Wettich seemingly confirmed their fears. Every time he tried to drive his animals past her house, they would get spooked and turn around. Eventually, Wettich was forced to take a different route altogether. The locals avoided the strange woman as much as possible.

In the Enon Valley area, more stories emerged. The area was heavily settled by German farmers. One evolved out of a neighborly dispute. It started with a farmer's daughter who had to cross her neighbor's field to get to the mailbox. One day, she encountered the farmer who lived on the other farm and said something that the man found offensive. His reaction was to immediately lash the girl several times with his whip. The girl's father was angry and took the neighbor to court. The judge ruled in his favor, but it's not clear what punishment the neighbor received. However, it seemed that the neighbor was not finished with the family yet. Shortly after the court case, strange things began to occur in the victorious farmer's house. Weird noises were heard all night. Locked doors would be found open, furniture overturned and dishes broken. Nothing was ever missing, so the family did not believe it was a series of robberies. Eventually, they came to believe the disturbances were supernatural in nature, so they visited a witch master for help. The witch master drew water from his spring, filled it with herbs and recited a German incantation over the water. He then instructed the family to take the water home and cut a cedar branch. They were to dip the branch in the water and sprinkle it over every doorway, window, chimney and opening in the house. After the family did this, the mysterious happenings ceased.

Jan Andrews gave Black another account of a woman who believed she had been hexed. The woman went to see a witch master, and her fears were confirmed. To break the hex, the witch master instructed her to clean her house "from cellar to attic" and save all the dirt she collected. She was then to sew a bag made of red flannel that had never been used for another purpose. The dirt and floor sweepings were to be placed in the bag along with fifteen pins. Six were to point down, and nine up. She was to tie the bag shut with a rope, hang it from a tree and beat it with a club. After the woman did this, the hex was removed and her life returned to normal.

Black also collected a story of a man named Pete Mays who could call up the devil. The story was relayed to her by Helen Cosgrove, who stated it took place in Big Beaver Township. Pete lived just north of Newport, on the "old McGoggin farm" along the Beaver River. Pete, who was an odd man, would tell people that he could conjure the devil on his farm. Of course, few believed him, but occasionally he could convince a skeptic to visit and see for themselves. One of these skeptics was Dr. Loyal Wilson, a surgeon from New Castle. Pete took Wilson by horse and buggy back to the area he called the proving grounds. Several other curious people followed the pair. After Pete began his ritual, which is never described, tremendous lightning and thunder began out of nowhere. It was accompanied by a sound described as "a great groaning and moaning as of a myriad souls in torment; and a horrifying rattling and clanking of chains." It seemed that even Pete panicked at this occurrence. He reportedly said, "I must have done something wrong this time. Run for your life!" All of the onlookers fled as fast as possible, and Dr. Wilson was from then on convinced that Pete Mays told the truth. After hearing of the incident, a man from Newport named Mr. Truby insisted it was all a hoax and that Dr. Wilson was gullible for believing it. So Pete, after working up the nerve, took Mr. Truby to the same spot. There was another terrifying display of thunder, lightning and the moans of the damned. Mr. Truby fled and never set foot on Pete Mays's farm again.

Another slightly amusing tale of witchcraft survives from the area of Venango County. It was passed along by Joseph Kean in 1879 for inclusion in the *History of Venango County*. Kean did not give an exact date or timeframe for the incident, though context clues indicate that it may have been in the 1840s. He did not use any real names, presumably because individuals involved were still living at the time.

The story begins with a young woman of "respectable parentage" from Sunville who was suffering from terrible fits and spasms. Kean described her as "partially deranged." She described hearing a roaring in her ears and seeing double during the fits. Though the young woman's family initially believed that she was suffering greatly from an illness, another theory started to take hold in the community. Certain neighbors, who Kean described as "better acquainted with evil spirits than others," were convinced that she was under a witch's spell.

Once the rumor started, it spread quickly through the community and to nearby Dempseytown. Discussing the witch became a daily occurrence, and enough community pressure built up that the family accepted it as a possibility. Soon, several witch masters came to treat the girl, usually accompanied by curious neighbors. They placed horseshoes over all the doors and knives at every window, but the witch still seemed to come anyway and the fits continued. A seventh son named George Shunk was brought in because it was thought he could harm the witch. When the young woman's fits commenced, he instructed her to point in the direction where she thought the invisible witch was located. Shunk, looking rather foolish, swung

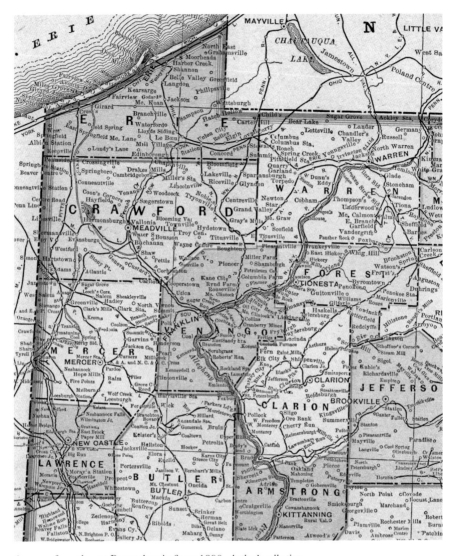

A map of northwest Pennsylvania from 1890. *Author's collection.*

a heavy club recklessly around the room at the girl's direction. He eventually conceded that he could not stop the witch.

On one occasion, a grizzled old veteran of the War of 1812 stepped forward and proclaimed that he did not fear the witch. He ordered the girl to fill a cup with water and drink it. She protested, claiming that the witch would prevent her from drinking. The veteran assured her that he could protect her, and the girl proceeded to drink. Afterward, she remained calm, with no fits. Instead of bringing an end to the situation, the others who witnessed the incident accused the veteran of practicing witchcraft and proceeded to harass him.

Soon another concerned neighbor suggested a possible solution. Since evil supernatural entities had difficulty crossing moving water, he suggested taking the girl across Sugar Creek by Dempseytown. Reluctantly, the puzzled family agreed, and the young woman was relocated. It was quickly evident that the tactic failed, and the fits soon continued. Some men speculated that the witch must have crossed via a rock or boulder and even searched the creek for the witch's path. A large hemlock tree that had fallen across the creek not far away was discovered, and to them, it confirmed their theory.

Back at the family's farmhouse, vigilant neighbors reported ominous black shapes and shadows lurking around the property. A well-known witch killer from Germany who now lived in Pennsylvania was sent for to drive off the witch. After several attempts, the often-intoxicated folk magician finally gave up, saying that American witches were too cunning. By now everyone in the region was talking about the strange case. Tensions escalated as things began to go wrong on other farms, such as outbreaks of disease among livestock and crop failures. Accusations flew as neighbor turned on neighbor. One Irish woman bore the brunt of the accusations. Just when things were getting out of hand, the accused began to file lawsuits against their accusers. The murmurings of witchcraft soon fell silent. As for the young woman, she sought treatment from a traditional physician and in a few weeks was fully recovered.

Warren County is located in the northwestern corner of the state, next to Erie County. In the early 1800s, the belief in witchcraft was so prevalent there that a man named John Meyers gained a reputation as a witch killer. Arch Bristol recorded most of what we know about Meyers, who lived along West Spring Creek until his death in 1821, in his book *Old Time Tales of Warren County*, published in 1932.

The ritual that Meyers used to kill witches has been documented and utilized by folk magic practitioners in the eastern and central parts of the state. Meyers was probably of German heritage himself and likely a powwower or hex doctor. When a bewitched person hired Meyers, he made them stand a few feet away from a long piece of paper that he had hung on the wall. He then lit a single candle in front of the person so their shadow was cast on the sheet of paper behind them. Carefully, Meyers would proceed to trace the outline of the shadow onto the paper. Next, he cut it out and adhered it to a wooden plank or board made of pine. Meyers would then take a silver bullet and load it in his gun with the smallest amount of gunpowder possible so the bullet could be recovered. The witch killer fired at the traced silhouette. It was believed that as the bullet passed through the paper, the witch would die, and any hex or curse that had been placed on the individual would be broken. A similar description of this witch killing method appeared in Joseph Doddridge's account of witchcraft.

Cases of witchcraft were not confined to the pre–Civil War era, nor were they confined to the countryside. In 1867, a woman from Pittsburgh named Mrs. Carr purchased a black cat in order to extract three drops of its blood. She gave them to a small child as a cure for croup. When her neighbors found out, they harassed the woman so badly that the authorities became involved. The woman was brought to court (though it's not clear if she was charged with anything or if her neighbors were), where she produced twenty witnesses who testified that the suffering child was instantly cured after her treatment.

In Indiana County, a hex doctor named Lincoln Wadding found himself in some legal trouble in 1888. He had advised a brother and sister from Dixonville, Rueben and Jane Black, that their recent troubles were a result of a witch. For a fee of $300, he offered to remove the witch's hex and protect them from further harm. They did not have the money, so he accepted a cow and a calf as payment. He performed some initial incantations and promised to return to finish the ritual. However, after he left with the animals, he did not return. The Blacks then had Wadding arrested, but the case was dropped after he agreed to return the cattle.

The rise of the spiritualist movement in the middle of the nineteenth century also provided more fodder for those looking for witches. In 1879, a twelve-year-old girl named Ella Huselton, who lived a few miles south of the city of Butler in Butler County, was either experiencing or was the source of spirit rappings. The girl was allegedly able to communicate with spirits by tapping and making noises. Some of her neighbors believed that the strange ability came about because the young lady was either possessed by an evil spirit or was in league with one. It was not long before several newspapers in Pittsburgh picked up the story, linking the girl to witchcraft. A second part of the story involves more traditional witchcraft ideas. George Huselton's nephew (the exact relationship to Ella is not clear) assaulted a farmhand on a neighboring farm where he worked. The attack was vicious enough that some locals believed he was either bewitched or possessed in some way. This may have been why Ella was trying to communicate with spirits. The family was not sure whether the nephew was just ill or really did have a supernatural oppressor, so they took him to a local witch master. That witch master recited several charms but was ultimately unable to help. He referred the family to another witch master who lived farther out in the country. This witch master prepared to extract the evil from the young man by cutting a large circle in the ground around a white oak tree. He performed a ceremony to draw out the evil from the boy and imprison it in the circle. He would do this alone with no spectators, though he warned a great noise resembling an army rushing through the forest might be heard, and the oak tree would be torn asunder. Unfortunately for us, the articles never mention whether the ceremony had any effect or if anyone heard the noise. The writer of an article in the *Somerset Herald* did mention that he learned of at least six witch masters who were active in Butler County at the time. In later accounts, the family denied that any witch masters were actually consulted.

Cases of alleged witchcraft and folk magic were reported well into the twentieth century. New immigrants brought supernatural traditions from southern and eastern Europe. Some of these are still passed through families today. The Great Migration of African Americans from the South around the time of the First World War brought more extensive traditions of Hoodoo to Pittsburgh and other northern urban centers. But these accounts are beyond the scope of this monograph. It should also be remembered that as time went on, especially by the Progressive era in the early twentieth century, the practice of folk magic was increasingly looked down on by the press, professional medicine and the "educated" public. Folk healing and witchcraft would come to be viewed as basically the same thing. Understanding of its nuances and the role it played for those who believed was lost for many of its critics.

Though it may seem that we have drifted away from Moll Derry's story in this chapter, it is necessary to look at the extent that the belief in witchcraft (and diabolical pacts) flourished in western Pennsylvania. These stories are only a sampling of the accounts of folk magic and healing prevalent in this region in the nineteenth century. It is the author's hope that these accounts will provide a better sense of context as we move on to examine the stories of Old Moll in more detail in the next chapter. It is important to note that Moll Derry was not the only witch in western Pennsylvania—she was just the most famous.

WHO WAS THE REAL MOLL DERRY?

Now that we have established a broader social context for the belief in witchcraft, it is possible to take a closer look at the specifics of Derry's life. Solid historical details about Moll Derry are far more elusive than tales of her magical abilities. Luckily, at least two members of the Derry clan have compiled genealogical records that will help us reconstruct at least some of Mary's life. The research of D. Doc Derry and Joan Brown Derry gives us a framework and context to examine the legends. Of course, there is not usually a lot of information available on most individuals from the 1700s and 1800s.

There is no known surviving record of Mary's birth, but it seems to have occurred between 1760 and 1768. It was probably closer to the former. According to family tradition, and later repeated in an 1879 newspaper article titled "The Mountain Hunter," which ran in several newspapers around the country, Mary Derry arrived in America with her husband, a Hessian mercenary soldier who was fighting for the British during the American Revolution. Women traveling with their soldier husbands was more common than we would assume today. There has been occasional disagreement as to her husband's name. Some believe that it was Jacob, because a Jacob Derry appears in tax records from 1785 in German Township, Fayette County. The fact that Mary had a son named Jacob would seem to support this. However, the previously mentioned 1879 article about the Derrys gives her husband's name as Valentine with a nickname of "Felty." Considering that more than half of the long article is about him, it would seem to be a critical error if it did not accurately record his name. The article also mentions Bazil Derry, another of Mary's sons, who died just before the time of publication. It is possible that he, his family or people who knew the Derrys well were sources. Of course, given the notorious inaccuracies in old newspapers, it is equally possible that the author relied purely on hearsay. For now though, I will simply refer to her husband as Valentine unless noted otherwise.

Sometime after their arrival, the Derrys decided to change sides, and Valentine reportedly joined General Daniel Morgan's sharpshooters/riflemen out of Virginia. Loudoun County, Virginia, was reported as the Derrys' home before they came to Pennsylvania. It should be noted that it has not been definitively proven that Valentine was one of Morgan's sharpshooters. He may have simply served under Morgan's command. "The Mountain Hunter" gives the following account:

> *Valentine Derry, commonly called Felty, and Mollie, his wife, came to Western Pennsylvania at the time of the Revolutionary War. They were both Haytiens* [an old spelling of Hessian] *and both belonged to the British army. Derry, with his wife, deserted and joined the American side and were under General Morgan. After the Declaration of Independence, Derry and his wife found their way over the mountains and settled in George's Township, Fayette County, Pa., took up a small tract of land at the foot of the mountains, about half a mile south of where old Pine Grove Forge used to stand. After building a cabin, Derry employed his after life exclusively in hunting deer and bear, in which he was remarkably successful. The deer and bear were plenty, and he never went without capturing just what he wanted.*

This account would seem to be clear enough; however, it left out what seems to be a brief residence in Bedford County, Pennsylvania. The Derrys might have lived there temporarily before moving to Fayette County, because their son Bazil was born there in 1786. (It should be noted that an alternate date for his birth is given in some sources as 1793.) Another unanswered question is what year they arrived in America. Since Mary's maiden name is unknown, and since her husband's first name is not definite, it is difficult to track their movement. Derry is likely the Americanized version of the surname Doering, which compounds the problem. Another descendant of the Derry family, Kathy Volpe Sawyer, believes that Mary may have been a member of the Ulrich family. It is possible that the couple arrived near the end of the Revolution, as late as 1783. Regardless of

Postcard from the early twentieth century showing George's Creek. The creek runs past many of the locations mentioned in the legends of Moll Derry. *Author's collection.*

when they arrived, we do know that they were living near Haydentown in Fayette County by the early 1790s.

It is interesting that the "Mountain Hunter" article indicates that Valentine also had a reputation for using folk magic to help him hunt. It described his supernatural talents as follows:

> *It was thought by many persons that he was a wizard, and could charm the deer. He sometimes used a certain ingredient that he rubbed on his moccasins and leggings. He would then make a circuit where the deer were plenty, and take his position some twenty-five or thirty steps at either side. In a short time he would see a buck coming at a slow trot. When at proper range he would bleat, the deer would stop, and he was always sure of his meat. If he wanted another one he never had to wait long.*

This short passage indicates that at least some people believed he used an enchanted salve or powder and possibly a special call to attract the deer and hold it in place. Also of note is the fact that he made a circle around the area where the deer were located. While he may have been just searching for a good position, he may also have been creating a magic circle.

One may wonder why Valentine and his hunting magic did not become a local legend or at least part of Old Moll's tales. There could be several reasons, including the fact that he seemed to have died long before Mary. The exact day or year of his death has not been discovered, but he is thought to have been born in the early 1750s, making him almost a decade older than Mary. From the few available sources, we can make a reasonable guess that he was dead before 1805. Another reason may be the fact that the stories about Mary are more interesting and dramatic. And of course, it could simply be the fact that she was a woman and therefore more likely to be associated with magic and witchcraft in the nineteenth century and by later writers and storytellers.

Though "The Mountain Hunter" was primarily about Valentine, the second half of the article focused on Mary. After referencing his wife, it said, "She was famous, not only in the neighborhood, but in places more remote, as a 'Fortune Teller.'" Clearly, Old Moll's reputation was well established, but not necessarily as a witch. It went on to say, "Young men and maidens and those of a more mature age and wisdom visited her mountain home in the hopes of hearing of something that would help them for either *weal* or *woe*." From the tone of the article, it seems that Mary was perceived as a helpful practitioner of folk magic, with the exception of one line near the end of the following quotation. The article continues to describe her work in more detail:

> *Was anything lost or stolen, whether horse or cow, pocket-book, money, jewels, silver spoons, or anything of real or imaginary value, the powers of this celebrated fortune-teller, having the well known name of Moll Derry, were frequently called into requisition. Many and miraculous were the stories treasured in the memory of the oldest inhabitants, and related for fireside entertainment, of her actually telling, without any hint, the article lost, when and where it would be found, and if stolen a description of the thief, whether male or female. Certain it is, if character be a test of truth, tradition has awarded to Moll Derry the title at least of being a remarkably good guesser. Her invariable dress was a short gown and petticoat, fabricated from the raw material, and by her own hand. Her method of unfolding the future destiny of her votaries was done through the simple medium of coffee.*

The parties seeking their fortunes had to take with them, in addition to money, a certain portion of the article first mentioned. This was prepared in the usual way, care being taken that it should be strong, and that a goodly quantity of the sediment or grounds should adhere to the sides and bottom of the cup. After the liquid had been leisurely sipped, Moll, during the sipping operation, would closely scan the visages of her subject, creating the impression that she was then in search after coming revelations. The cup being placed in the left hand of the seeker, bottom upwards, and the subject required to turn the cup three times, being careful to turn the cup toward the seeker, Moll would then take the cup, and by the grounds that adhered to the sides and bottom, read off the seeker's fortune. It was thought by many that Moll had intimate dealings with the devil. As far as known, she harmed no one, and if she got her money and her coffee, she was always contented.

This account of Mary is interesting, not only because it describes what people remembered as a typical interaction with her for supernatural guidance and details about her fortune telling method, but also for the seemingly out-of-place line near the end that ties her to the devil. Only a generation after her death, Moll Derry still had a dual reputation as being both helpful yet linked to evil at the same time. This article also confirms historically, if it is indeed accurate, that Mary was really as well known for her supernatural dealings as the legends say.

One thing that is apparent is that the Derry family was probably not very wealthy. Though they had land in the mountains, they did not have a true farm in any sense. (This land was around the conveniently named Derry Hill today.) Mary's only documented sources of income were telling fortunes and selling small amounts of whiskey, while Valentine was a professional hunter. In that way, they were similar to many of the poor families that settled in the Appalachians (both North and South) in the years of the early republic. Moll's activities would certainly supplement their relatively meager

Sketch of Moll Derry inspired by the legends. *Courtesy of Tom J. White.*

income. This is not to imply that Moll was some type of con artist. It is very likely that she and her neighbors truly believed in her supernatural abilities, so the transaction was merely perceived as paying for a service.

Together, Valentine and Mary managed to support their seven children. Bazil was the eldest, followed by Jacob, Barbara, Philip, Jeremiah, Rhoda and Mary. It was Bazil who would follow his father's example and become a well-known hunter (who also made shoes and burned charcoal for furnaces in Haydentown). In 1812, he married Mary Schultz, and they purchased some land nearby in Georges Township. Bazil lived a long time, until May 20, 1879, so some stories about him appeared in local newspapers. One article, titled "The Old Hunter," appeared shortly before his death in the *Daily Standard*:

> *Bazil Derry was born in Bedford County, Pa., in the month of April 1786, and is now 92 years of age. His wife, Mary, was born in the same county, in the year 1789, and is now 90 years of age. The venerable couple have lived in the same house nearly 70 years, about ½ mile south of Wood's Tannery, and near the foot of the mountain in Georges Township.*
>
> *Mr. Derry has been confined to his bed for 8 months, is reduced to a mere skeleton, and is almost blind. They had five children born to them, all who are living: Jacob, their only son, is over 60 years old age; Mrs. John Gates, Mrs. Samuel Huntley, Mrs. William Emme, and Mrs. George Hartman, are their daughters. They have a large number of grandchildren and several great-grandchildren.*
>
> *Mr. Derry was a shoemaker by trade, but followed hunting in the mountains until his eyesight failed, and it is safe to say that he has caught more coon, and shot more turkeys and squirrels, and killed more rattlesnakes, than any other man that lived in Fayette County. He has been to the head of the Cheat River, and all over the Canaan Valley on that stream in his hunting tours.*
>
> *Mr. Derry is a very singular and eccentric man, is entirely unlettered, but well acquainted with the habits and instincts of wild animals.*

After reading such an article, one could justifiably speculate that Bazil likely continued to practice some of the hunting folk magic traditions of his father, in addition to just being an excellent hunter. The article makes no mention of his locally well-known parents, however. Another lengthier article appeared over a decade after his death in the *Genius of Liberty*. The article talks about the hunting prowess of not only Bazil, but also his wife,

Postcard showing the banks of the Cheat River, one of Bazil Derry's hunting grounds. *Author's collection.*

Mary, and tells the story of their early life together. Its title was "A Couple Who Slew Wild Animals About Haydentown in Early Days." The sources for the article were several people who "knew them well." Their names are given as J. Gates Hartman (who would have been a relative) and A.W. Scott. The article also quotes another old hunter, Url Parmly, who was only seven years younger than Bazil. Parmly's tales of the couple's hunting ability began on their wedding day. He said:

> *The day they were married they started afoot through the woods on their wedding tour to their new home in the mountains. Basil carried his rifle and on the way to, killed 15 wild turkeys, 5 deer, a bear and 2 wildcats. The bear and the wildcats Basil and his wife hung up in the woods out of the reach of wolves, and he shouldered 2 deer and 6 of the turkeys and his wife loaded herself with the 9 remaining turkeys and carried them to their home. Some of the burden had to be carried 20 miles.*

He continues, relating how they marched back into the woods after dropping off their kills to fetch the bear and wildcats. Bazil sold the turkeys and the bearskin in Haydentown, earning the young couple some extra money. Parmly also relates that Bazil was a good fiddler and was asked to stay and play his fiddle for a while. In another paragraph, he relayed more personal information about Bazil:

> *When out hunting Derry always wore moccasins made by himself out of a groundhog skin. He made his way through the woods on these as noiselessly as a shadow. He had two guns, both flint locks, and he never changed them to percussion locks when those were invented. He called his guns "Burnt Eye" and "Black Snake." "Black Snake" he always kept at home for his wife in emergencies. In case no emergency arose she frequently started out herself in the woods to raise one. She seldom came back home without a turkey or two, perhaps a deer and likely as not a bear.*

Though the entire article continues to focus on the hunting skills of the couple, Parmly states near the end that Bazil was the son of Molly Derry, the Fortune Teller of the Revolution.

Bazil may have remained in Fayette County, but some of Mary's children eventually moved west. Jacob Derry and his family moved to Indiana, then later Illinois. But Mary stayed put on the mountain, presumably doing what she had always done, reading fortunes and selling a little whiskey. We know very little about her final years and probable decline in health, but she must have seen the end coming. On May 15, 1843, she compiled her final will. By June 17, she was dead. The will has survived and is reproduced here:

> *1843 Last Will and Testament of Mary Derry of Georges Township Fayette County*
>
> *In the name of God, I, Mary Derry, considering the uncertainty of the mortal life and being of sound mind and memory, blessed be almighty God for the same, do make this my last will and testament in manner and form following that is to say, first I give and bequeath unto my grandchild Andrew Derry, the son of Mary Fowler, the house and lot where I now live in Haydentown or George Town, lying and being in George's Township in Fayette County and state above mentioned it being the whole of my freehold estate whatsoever to hold him, the said Andrew Derry, his heirs and assigns forever, whom I hereby appoint Mary Fowler sole Executrix of this my last will and testament, hereby revoking all former wills by me made. In witness whereof I have hereunto set by my hand and seal the fifteenth day of May*

in the year of our Lord, one thousand eighteen hundred and forty-three.
Attested by Jacob Dawson and Jacob Derry
(Will proved 17 of June, 1843, Jacob Dawson testified before Joseph
Gadd, Registrar for the probate, that the will of Mary Derry, late of
George Township, is as it is purported to be.)

Unless more sources are discovered, the previous information would seem to be the only historical information available about Mary Derry. To learn more about the nature of the Witch of the Monongahela, we will have to turn to less reliable sources—the legends themselves. Legends may not always be factually true, but they often reflect some truth at their core. We can also learn a great deal from the way they are transmitted, as every storyteller leaves an individual mark.

A CLOSER LOOK
AT THE LEGENDS

E ven though the historical records are sparse, there is at least some verifiable framework in which to place Derry's life in early western Pennsylvania. Now it is time to circle back and reexamine the legends about the Witch of the Monongahela within this context. Though these legends have been passed on by word of mouth and in print for nearly two centuries by many different writers and storytellers, they appear to have retained much consistency in their content and form. Still, this does not mean that the legends did not evolve over time and that the context in which they were told did not change. Tales of Moll Derry that were recounted by word of mouth, especially in the early years, are lost to us. These likely included many more stories and accounts of personal interactions that have disappeared or have survived only as a short synopsis or kernel narrative. We are left with only the written record to guide us as to the evolution of the legends. Written sources alone create an incomplete picture when it comes to folklore, but they are all we have. Each of the four main stories from the first chapter has its own set of written sources behind it, but there was one writer who compiled most of these stories in the twentieth century and brought them to a larger audience. Before we examine the background of each legend individually, let us take a brief look at the life and work of the prolific George Swetnam.

George Francis Swetnam was born just outside of Cincinnati, Ohio, on March 11, 1904. His family would move to several different southern states in his youth, and he obtained several different degrees from prominent universities, including the University of South Carolina, the University of

Alabama and the University of Mississippi. He earned bachelor's degrees in English and theology, a master's degree in theology and a doctorate in Assyriology. During his studies, he learned to speak German and to read ancient cuneiform. Swetnam was also an ordained Presbyterian minister. Throughout his life, he worked at various times as a journalist, photographer, college professor, historian and folklorist. While living in Pennsylvania, he helped to start the Institute of Pennsylvania Rural Life and Culture in Lancaster. In 1943, he settled with his family in the Pittsburgh suburb of Glenshaw and began writing and editing for the *Pittsburgh Press*. He was known for his articles on the history and folklore of the region and eventually wrote several books, including *Pittsylvania Country* (1951), which includes an account of Moll Derry. He also served as editor of *Keystone Folklore Quarterly* from 1959 to 1965. After retiring in 1973, he continued to write occasionally and published additional books. One of these, published in 1988, was *Devils, Ghosts, and Witches: Occult Folklore of the Upper Ohio Valley*, which again incorporates stories about Moll Derry. Swetnam passed away on April 3, 1999.

Interestingly, throughout the 1960s at least, he also maintained correspondence with several contemporary practitioners of folk magic. It seems this began after he wrote an article about a modern witchcraft practitioner for the *Pittsburgh Press*. Though the paper generally did not like to run articles on the occult, Swetnam was allowed on that occasion. It seems that this article resulted in him being contacted by several witches who wished to discuss magic and witchcraft in greater detail.

Since Swetnam's writings in the 1950s and 1980s served as the basis for our modern accounts, we will work backward from these to try to learn what we can about the legends. We will also look at the writings of a few other authors who were key to building the story of Moll Derry and discuss their work as it is reached. Following the same order in which the stories were presented earlier in the book, the legend of the three hanged men will be addressed first.

Though this story is one of the most frequently repeated ones about Moll Derry, Swetnam did not address it in his later writings. However, it was featured in his brief write-up on Derry in *Pittsylvania Country*. Before looking at his account, it will be beneficial to look at his description of Moll Derry from the same source. He described her as a "stooped, aged hag, of whom all that now remains certain is that she had a ghastly reputation as a witch such as was never attached to the name of any other woman in the Pittsylvania Country." This statement is interesting for two reasons.

George Swetnam's books that include sections on Moll Derry. *Author's collection.*

First, Swetnam describes Derry in rather sinister terms, firmly framing her as a traditional witch. Second, it is clear that, at least at the time of this 1951 writing, he is unaware of other substantial cases of alleged witchcraft in western Pennsylvania (what he calls Pittsylvania), stating that no other woman had such a reputation. As we saw in the previous chapter, allegations of witchcraft were not as rare as one would suspect, and although none of the other witches developed quite the level of infamy in modern times, they were better known in the nineteenth century. In fact, it can and will be argued as we proceed that it was actually Swetnam who amplified Derry's reputation as the "lone" witch of southwestern Pennsylvania. This is understandable considering that Swetnam was not a native to the region and was still learning and researching its historical intricacies. *Pittsylvania Country* was a successful book and can still be found in numerous Pennsylvania libraries and used bookstores. For many people, it was their first (and perhaps only) exposure to the story of Moll Derry.

Returning to the three hanged men, Swetnam leads into his account by describing how women who crossed Derry would find that their bread did not rise. The only way to end this curse was to heat and then cool a horseshoe and hang it above the door. He continued, "Legend said, too, that Moll once placed a curse on three men who made fun of her, telling them that all three would be hanged." The story went on:

> *One was John McFall, who pulled a tavern door from its hinges in 1795 and bludgeoned the keeper to death in a drunken rage. He was the first man ever hanged in Fayette County. A second was Ned Cassidy, who fled West after a peddler was butchered and sunk in a millpond in 1800. In Ohio he murdered another man and was hanged. But first he signed a confession to the murder of the peddler, which was mailed back to Uniontown by those who hung him. The third, whose name is not preserved, went to Greene County and hanged himself in a fit of despondency, according to the legend.*

As one can see, this is essentially the story as it is told today. This account was reproduced almost verbatim in a 1972 article by Joseph G. Smith in *Western Pennsylvania Historical Magazine*. Titled "Ruffians, Robbers, Rogues, Rascals, Cutthroats, and Other Colorful Characters," the article reintroduced Derry to new readers and added a layer of academic credibility to Swetnam's account. In 1976, the *Uniontown Morning Herald* ran an article on witches in Fayette County, and the story was repeated again in a shorter form.

One of the frustrating things about Swetnam's writing on Moll Derry is that we do not always know what his direct sources were. Two different collections of his personal papers have survived and are publicly accessible, and although they include much of his research, neither contains his documentation on Moll Derry. It is likely that he drew most of his information from old local histories and newspaper articles, as well as from interviews with people who heard the stories growing up in Fayette County.

Wherever Swetnam got his information, it is clear that the story was in circulation for a long time. A fictionalized version appeared in Alonzo F. Hill's book *The White Rocks: or, The Robbers' Den. A Tragedy of the Mountains*. Hill's book is a fictional version of the story of Polly Williams and her murder. In this version, Moll Derry is given the name Molly Pry. Though she was deceased by the time of the book's publication in 1865, her children were not, and that is why many believe the name was changed. In fact, many historical figures in the book have their names altered. In the discussion of Molly Pry that occurs between Mary (Polly) and her cousin Tilly, the story of the hanged men comes up. When Tilly mentions that she would rather not run into Moll Pry, Mary asks:

"Why so? She was never known to harm anyone."

"No, not directly; but if she predicts evil of any one it is sure to come to pass; and that is what I should fear—that she might say some horrid things of my future. Three men once, of the names of Butler, Dougherty and Flanigan, of whom you have no doubt heard—"

"Yes, I have heard of them."

"Well they were up in the mountain after chestnuts, and they met old Molly, and provoked her in some way, and she cursed them, and predicted that they would all be hung before a year. She came pretty near the truth, if not quite. Butler was hung for killing and robbing a drover before six months—the only man ever hung in Fayette County; Dougherty shot a man over in Greene County, and was hung by a mob before the year was up, and Flanigan, about the same time, murdered his wife with an ax, and ran away to escape justice. It is not known positively that Molly's prediction was verified in this case, though it has been rumored that he fled to Ohio, and shortly after, in a crazy fit, brought on by drink, hung himself in a barn."

"I have heard of those men, and of their deeds, but I was not aware that old Molly warned them of their fate."

"She had though; for they stopped at our house on their way home and took dinner, and they laughingly told father of their adventure with the old woman, how they had teased and taunted her to hear her swear, and how she had prophesied that they should all be hung before the chestnuts should be ripe again. It was ten years ago, and I was quite young then, but I remember it distinctly."

Hill's account is more detailed than most but is also very different. This is of course due to the fact that many of the names of actual individuals were changed in the book, though their general stories remain fairly accurate. Aside from the different set of names and the differences in details of the crimes, the core of the story is still the same—three men taunted her and she cursed them to hang. Her prediction came true. Hill added the final part as firsthand confirmation of Moll Pry's (Derry's) power to emphasize the importance of her subsequent prediction to Mary/Polly. We will return to Hill's account when we discuss Derry's part in the story of Polly Williams.

Before Hill's fictionalized version, it does not seem that we have any surviving direct written accounts of the story of the three hanged men. It is possible that Hill fabricated the story for dramatic effect, but that does not explain the different set of names used in most accounts. Generally, Hill adapted local happenings in the book, so there is just as much of a chance (if not more) that Derry's curse on the men was an authentic part of local folklore. So now we must ask—what, if anything, do we know about the men mentioned in the story?

In all but Hill's account, the first of the men to face the noose was John McFall. Luckily, there is historical information available about McFall, who was a real person. He really was the first man ever hanged in Fayette County. Early on the morning of November 10, 1794, McFall murdered innkeeper John Chadwick in Smithfield. The two had been arguing earlier when McFall threatened to kill a constable named Myers (who had previously arrested him) inside the inn. When Chadwick intervened, McFall threatened him too. Myers decided to leave and went outside to his horse. McFall followed him out and continued arguing. When Myers rode off, he tried to return to the inn, but Chadwick would not let him back in and ordered him to go home. Feigning acceptance, McFall shook his hand and walked away. Only minutes later, he charged back to the door and tore it off its hinges. He grabbed Chadwick, dragged him outside and proceeded to beat him with a club until his skull was cracked. Chadwick clung to life for almost two days before dying in agony.

A photo of the old Nixon Tavern near Fairchance taken in 1934. This tavern was similar to the tavern in Smithfield where John McFall murdered John Chadwick. *Courtesy of the Library of Congress, Prints and Photographs Division.*

After the murder, McFall fled to Virginia, but he was captured and returned to Uniontown. He was quickly put on trial and convicted of first-degree murder. His sentence was death. Before it could be implemented, he escaped from prison but was apprehended again near Hagerstown. In May 1795, he was hanged in a clearing near Redstone Creek close to Fairchance.

Ned Cassidy, the second man, was also a real person. We will return to him and his associate John Updyke shortly when we discuss the legend of the murdered peddler. For now though, we can confirm that he did help murder the peddler sometime after 1800, fled west to somewhere in Ohio and committed a second murder. Before he was hanged for that murder, he wrote a confession to the peddler's murder that was sent back to Fayette County (at least according to the 1882 *History of Fayette County*).

So that brings us to two confirmed hangings. Unfortunately, all of the accounts aside from Hill's fictionalized version never name the third man. There is no way to verify whether this individual really traveled to Greene County and hanged himself. It seems that if Derry really did curse the men to hang as the legend claims, then at least part of what she predicted came to pass. Of course, there are no early historical sources that document her interaction with the men. But it would be highly unusual for such an occurrence to be written into a history book in the 1800s. This leaves open the possibility that it did occur. It simply may have been a neighborhood dispute that took on legendary status due to the individuals involved and the seemingly accurate nature of Derry's predictions. After all, an argument between an alleged witch and several shady characters would not likely be forgotten.

Of course, another possibility is that Hill did fabricate or exaggerate the encounter for his book and later writers assumed it was based on a real account. They may have tried to figure out who the real figures were and assigned McFall and Cassidy to the roles. While this is possible, it seems unlikely, because Hill makes the point that "Butler" was the only man ever hanged in Fayette County. At that point in time, McFall was still the only man to be hanged in Fayette County, and his story was well known. It seems that Hill was just letting the reader know exactly who Butler was supposed to represent, considering he changed details of the crimes. One could argue that it is possible that Hill used known criminals as the inspiration for the characters but still made up the encounter with the witch. That, too, is a possibility, but he did rely heavily on local folklore throughout his account. Given Derry's reputation, it seems likely that there was some kind of dispute that the encounter with the three men would have been at least loosely based on. Unfortunately, unless an earlier written account of the legend turns up in the future, we will never know for certain.

A closer look at the related legend of the murdered peddler yields no more definitive information than that of the three hanged men. Swetnam wrote about Ned Cassidy and the murdered peddler in *Devils, Ghosts, and Witches*. This was his final writing on Derry, but the details are somewhat different from what would be expected. Cassidy's name is now spelled Casedy, and the year of the murder is changed from shortly after 1800 to "the late spring of 1818 or 1819." According to Swetnam, a peddler from New Jersey visited a tavern kept by Nace Kyle. There he met John Updyke, who was also originally from New Jersey and happened to be an old acquaintance. Updyke invited him to his house, and though he initially hesitated, the peddler agreed to go. Along the way, they met Updyke's friend Ned Casedy and decided to have a few more drinks. They passed by Updyke's home outside of Smithfield, near Ruble's Mill, and walked to Haydentown to drink whiskey. Then it was decided to travel to Moll Derry's dwelling to a dance. Why a dance was occurring at Moll Derry's house is not explained, although perhaps it had to do with her sale of whiskey. It was also emphasized that she was a fortune teller, implying that the peddler might want his fortune told. The three men left, but instead of going to see Moll Derry, Updyke and Casedy took him back toward Updyke's home. Somewhere along the way, the pair attacked and murdered the peddler. The next morning, a man named Robert Brownfield found a bloody handprint near Updyke's home and followed a trail of blood across Robert Collin's farm to the hill above Weaver's Mill dam and pond. It is presumed the body was found in the pond at some point, but it is not explicitly stated. Suspicion immediately fell on Casedy and Updyke, but neither was arrested in spite of the circumstantial evidence.

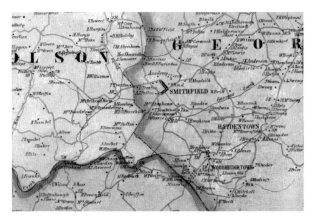

An 1858 map of Fayette County depicting the area around Haydentown and Smithfield. Weaver's Mill is visible on the map. *Courtesy of the Library of Congress, Prints and Photographs Division.*

Shortly after the murder, Updyke became ill. One day, a "respectable citizen of George" named Valentine Moser was visiting Updyke's neighbor Hannah Clarke. Clarke was known locally as a witch, and when Moser arrived, she showed him a drawing on the back of her door. It was an outline of John Updyke, with a nail tapped into the side of the head and one at the left temple. She explained that if she drove the nails into the drawing the entire way, Updyke would die, but instead she tapped them in a little every day to torture him. Swetnam continued:

> *Updyke, after a lingering illness, died; during his sickness, refusing to sleep at night, unless a light was burning and someone sat by the bedside and held his hand. People said his terrible painful sickness and death was a judgement upon him for killing the pedlar.*

Swetnam then described Ned Casedy's visit to Moll Derry, where he asked for "something that would put a fellow to sleep." He continued, "Old Mollie fastened her keen piercing eyes on him and asked him why he came to her for potion when his hands were not yet dry from committing murder." Casedy was taken aback by her statement and turned and quickly walked away.

Once again, Swetnam's account is basically the version that circulates on the internet and in print today. The question is, where did he obtain such a detailed account? Luckily, this time he had a single footnote that points to the source. The account came from an article titled "The Black Gang" in the newspaper the *Genius of Liberty*. Published on July 14, 1881, the article was written by the prominent local historian Samuel T. Wiley. Born in 1850, Wiley overcame many challenges, including severe physical injuries, to become a writer and educator. He eventually authored dozens of books on the history of various counties and regions in Pennsylvania.

Wiley began the article discussing how criminal gangs moved west after the American Revolution and how the young Ned Casedy "eagerly drank in" stories of these gangs and "signaled his arrival at the years of manhood by separating a man and his wife." He describes Casedy as attending every horse race and chicken fight in the area as well as drinking, gambling and fighting, thereby "rapidly gaining for himself the character of a bad and dangerous man." He also operated a still and stole clothing from clotheslines and meat from smokehouses. Casedy would harass all but the strongest men in the county, picking fights and stealing property.

From there, Wiley launches into the account of the murdered peddler. It is clear that Swetnam reproduced Wiley's account almost exactly. However, there is one minor difference that substantially changes Casedy's reason for approaching Old Moll. In Swetnam's telling, Derry asks why he came to her for potion, which initially just seems like an awkwardly worded response. Potion does not seem out of place, because it is a witch story after all. But, in the original article by Wiley, Derry says poison instead of potion. It could be implied from Swetnam's account that perhaps Casedy was having trouble sleeping because of guilt or perhaps it was for Updyke who was suffering and getting worse. Instead, Casedy was looking to commit another murder, or at least do something devious. Perhaps he even meant to kill Updyke before he could confess to the murder.

In fact, that is exactly what is put forth in Franklin Ellis's *History of Fayette County, Pennsylvania*. Published in 1882, just a year after Wiley's article, it also gives a short account of the murdered peddler story in addition to the account of the McFall murder that we previously mentioned. Ellis used the spelling Cassidy throughout his description, which leaves out Hannah Clarke and Moll Derry entirely. His account of the murder (said to take place shortly after 1800) is similar to Wiley's, but his description of the fate of the men includes nothing supernatural. He explains:

> *Updyke and Cassidy were never arrested. Soon after Updyke was taken down with a loathsome disease, which was said to have been superinduced by poison given him by Cassidy, who was afraid that Updyke would divulge the crime or turn State's evidence. He soon died a most horrible death. Ned Cassidy went West as soon as Updyke had died. He there committed another murder, for which he was tried, convicted, and before being executed he made a confession, in which he stated that he and Updyke had murdered the peddler, and after securing a handsome sum of money they sank his body in Brownfield's mill-dam. William Sturgis has the confession.*

So we have two accounts, published roughly a year apart, about the same crime. One contains witches, and the other does not. How can these accounts be reconciled? And what does the fact that Casedy/Cassidy approached Moll Derry for poison say about her? One of the first discrepancies between the two accounts is the date. Wiley's "spring of 1818 or 1819" sounds like it came from a personal recollection. We do not know Wiley's source or sources, but given the type and amount of detail in his account, it seems likely that it came directly from people

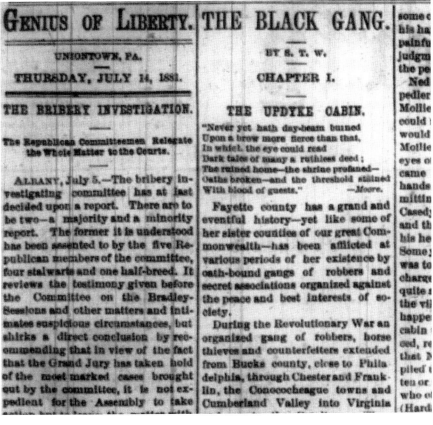

The article "The Black Gang" appeared in the *Genius of Liberty* in 1881. It was George Swetnam's source for the story of the murdered peddler. *Author's collection.*

who remembered the incident or were told the story by someone who did. Ellis's date is vague and his account more traditional. "Shortly after 1800" can represent a wide range of years, depending on who you ask. It may seem like a stretch to us to call 1818 shortly after 1800, but it depends on context. Given that Ellis could not come up with a specific date either, it seems to indicate a lack of written sources and reliance on oral tradition. If 1818 or 1819 was the date of the incident, it creates new problems for interpreting the other legends. First, it would create a large gap of over twenty years between McFall's hanging and Cassidy's hanging in the legend of the three hanged men. It is doubtful that anyone would pay attention to or put stock in the curse after that much time. Secondly, in the fictionalized account of Polly Williams's murder (which occurred in reality in 1810) by Hill, all three hanged men were already dead. This would mean that the legend of the hanged men was in circulation before 1810, if it was in fact an authentic legend. If not, it may have been fabricated by Hill or only became a community legend much later. Hill's book was published in 1865, so it may have incorporated legends that developed in the intervening years that were believed to have been true. It is important to note, however, that Ellis places the story of the murdered peddler chronologically before the death of Polly Williams.

A clue can be found in the same location as the peddler's body. The millpond may help us narrow down the timeframe. Though today the body is often said to have been found at Ruble's Mill near Updyke's and Derry's homes, it was actually discovered at another nearby mill mentioned in Wiley's and Ellis's accounts. Brownfield's Mill and Weaver's Mill, mentioned in Ellis and Wiley, respectively, are the same location. Brownfield was the original owner, and it was Weaver's Mill at the time of Wiley's article. According to Ellis, Charles Brownfield built the mill around 1806. This means the murder had to have occurred after that. It is just speculation, but if the murder actually occurred in 1808 or 1809 instead of the reported 1818 or 1819 (which seemed to be based off of someone's recollection rather than documentation), then the story of the three hanged men might have been circulating by 1810. In that case, almost all of the elements of both accounts could have been true. Cassidy may have very well been poisoning Updyke at the same time the mysterious Hannah Clarke cursed him. Cassidy would have had time to commit another murder in Ohio and confess before the death of Polly Williams. Unfortunately, we do not know where in Ohio that Cassidy went. If he could be located there, then a more precise date might be determined. Regardless, by the 1870s, versions of these legends circulated with contradictory dates.

This brings us to Derry's appearance as Moll Pry in the tale of Polly Williams. Sadly, the death of Mary "Polly" Williams at the White Rocks is a true story. The only part that cannot be verified is the encounter with Moll Derry. Polly Williams's body was discovered at the base of the White Rocks in 1810 after falling over sixty feet. She was to meet Philip Rogers on May 12 because they were supposed to be married. Unlike the legend, Williams did not know that they were going to the White Rocks but thought they were headed to Woodbridgetown. Rogers suggested the last-minute detour. After the body was found, Rogers admitted they argued at the rocks, but he had left, implying that she was confused and must have accidentally fallen over the cliff. It was clear that her death was no accident, because it was

This 1906 postcard is a photograph taken from the base of the White Rocks where Polly Williams's body was found. The writing on the card mentions the murder. *Author's collection.*

discovered that she sustained a blow to the head before the fall. There were also signs of a struggle near the edge of the cliff. Rogers's family hired the prominent Pittsburgh attorney Senator James Ross to defend him after his arrest. Though most believed Rogers to be guilty, it could not be proven in court, so he was released. With a tarnished reputation, he moved to Greene County and lived into his seventies.

The tragedy was talked about for many years and inspired poems, short stories and Hill's embellished account. A gravestone is maintained to this day for Polly in White Rocks Cemetery, and sometimes people claim to see her ghost nearby or at the White Rocks. Several of the early writings about the murder were gathered and preserved in Frank Cowan's 1878 book *Southwestern Pennsylvania in Song and Story*. (We will talk more about Cowan shortly.) Poems such as "The Hoary Old Hero of Hell," "Polly Williams" and "The Murder of Polly Williams" (the latter by A.F. Hill) capture the emotional impact and outrage that was felt in the community after the crime. But none of these accounts includes an encounter with Moll Derry/Pry. It appears that the first time that the encounter was described in print was Hill's *The White Rocks*. Previously, we examined how Mary (Polly) and Tilly discuss Derry/Pry's reputation, but now we will look at her role in the rest of the story.

Immediately after Mary and Tilly talk about Moll Pry and the three hanged men, Mary asserts that she would still like to meet her to have her fortune told. The young women talk briefly, speculating that Moll Pry could tell them about their future husbands. The pair then walk up to the White Rocks and continue their discussion, soon stumbling upon Moll Pry standing on the edge of the cliff. She is described as follows:

> It is Molly Pry, the well-known fortune-teller of the mountain, who has, on many occasions, given proof of a strange power to tell of past events, and foretell those to come. Her appearance, as she stands there, is miserable, squalid and wretched, not to say frightful. She is about five feet high and very thin—almost a skeleton. Her apparel consists of nothing but rags from head to foot—miserable, colorless, dirty rags. The coarse black hair hangs in tangled masses from her head, which is entirely void of any artificial covering. Her cheeks are hollow and sunken, and her small black eyes are set deep in her head, and they glance out in such a disagreeable way, that one feels as uneasy in front of them as though they were the muzzles of loaded pistols.

As the young women stare, Moll Pry asks them what they are afraid of and, looking at Mary, says, "Ye can't fall over the rock while I'm standin' on this spot, though ye may when I'm not hur to watch ye." It is an ominous foreshadowing of Mary's fate. The young women explain that they were startled because they didn't expect anyone to be there. Moll continues, "Well, ye needn't fear me. I was never knowed to hurt nobody what didn't do me no harm. My name's Molly Pry; d'ye ever hear o' me?" Mary's reply starts a brief exchange that contains the most famous lines of the book. Mary says, "I think I have, you can tell fortunes can't you?" Moll answers, "Yes, an' *mis*-fortunes too." Mary replies, "Oh, I hope you wouldn't tell *me* any misfortunes." Assertively, Moll states, "I'll tell you the truth; I'll tell ye what's past and what's to come. Gi' me yer hand."

The text goes on to describe Mary's fear of pulling her hand away and her fear of breaking eye contact with Moll's piercing eyes. Moll first describes the gruesome death of her father in the past (tied to another part of the text) and then moves on to forecast her future. Moll says, "I'll tell you of love; yes love; plenty o' love—for you, all for you—love, fun, happiness, enjoyment, followed by—[there is a brief interruption from Mary]—Sickness, sadness, horror, murder, blood—yes, *blood*."

Mary withdraws her hand and sits back on the rock, looking pale. Moll moves on to Tilly, saying it is not as bad for her. Referencing Mary, she asserts, "*Your* father wasn't murdered, nor *you* ain't to be dashed to pieces among the rocks." Moll proceeds to warn Tilly that at some time in the future she would reject her lover, who would subsequently drown himself in the river. As both young women reel from the revelations, Moll tells them death is not so bad and hands Mary a flower that had been growing on the very edge of the cliff. Using the flower as a metaphor for Mary herself, Moll passes on one final warning before departing:

> *Ah, he tried hard to dash it down upon the rocks below, but he couldn't. Beware of him! He may yit! It is a tender plant, and in his rough grasp the blood would start from it and rouse the vengeance of the people there! Then more blood would flow! Blood! Blood! Blood! Beware of him! Beware!*

Mary and Tilly try to convince themselves that Moll Pry is simply crazy. Of course, later in the book Moll is proven correct about Mary's fate. The young woman is thrown down from the very spot where they had their conversation. This fateful encounter is not Moll Pry's last appearance in the book, however. In a later chapter, she saves Ned

Stanton after he is bitten by a rattlesnake. Stanton is attempting to twirl the rattlesnake above his head and toss it when the snake strikes his hand. As his friends watch in shock, Moll suddenly emerges out of the woods and moves in to help. She exclaims, "Stand aside, ye fools. What would become o' that man if I want' hur. Ha! Ha! Molly's never fur off when she's wanted—for all she's a wicked creature!" Moll quickly drops to the ground and grabs Ned's hand. Pulling it to her mouth, she begins to suck out the poison. She does this repeatedly until all the poison is drawn out. When she is finished, Moll explains that the poison couldn't hurt her because she has no teeth and her gums had long since healed over, so the poison could not get in her blood if she spit it out.

After a moment or two, Ned asks Moll what he could do for her in return for helping him. Moll says he did not need to do anything except stay away from snakes. Then she states that some people call her a devil, but if she were a devil, why would she save a man's life. Then she reveals that it was she who was returning a favor. Ned had forgotten, but when he was a boy, he once saw an old woman fall on some rocks. He had stopped to pick her up and walk her home. That old woman was, of course, Moll Pry. Before she disappears back into the woods, she says, "Molly may remember an *injury* for a *long time*; but a *kindness* she will *never* forgit. Good-by, an' don't fool with rattlesnakes anymore."

So what can we learn about Moll Derry from Hill's account? The unfortunate answer is nothing definitive. Hill may have relied heavily on local history and folklore, essentially keeping real people and changing their last names, but he also merged unrelated legends for the sake of the story. Part of the story involves outlaws hiding at Delaney's Cave (Laurel Caverns). While real criminals did hide in the cave at various points in the 1800s, they were not actually connected to Philip Rogers in any way. In Hill's book, Philip is secretly a leader of the outlaws who actually murdered Mary's (Polly) father. As we can see, this makes it difficult to determine whether Derry actually encountered Polly to warn her about her death at the White Rocks or if it was just another local legend intertwined in the tale for dramatic effect. It is clear though that Moll is viewed primarily as a fortune teller rather than a witch in the story. Her association with rattlesnakes is also expressed in her second appearance in the text.

Albert Bolen wrote an interesting fictional epilogue for the Moll Derry/ Polly Williams story in 1916. On January 19, the short story "Mountaineer's Tale" appeared in the *Morning Herald*. The story begins with the narrator, the mountaineer, walking along the Laurel Ridge on a bleak and ominous

A postcard from the early twentieth century showing another angle of the White Rocks in Fayette County. *Author's collection.*

late fall day. After two paragraphs describing feelings of melancholy and foreboding, the mountaineer spots another man walking ahead in the same direction. Thinking that his company would make the journey less dismal, he increases his pace to catch up with him. The slender man is unfriendly and described as being about seventy years old, with white hair and a beard. He looks around frequently and appears nervous. Nothing is said as the mountaineer walks along beside him. After about fifteen minutes, they spot a decrepit old woman holding up a panther cub by the neck under a tree near the road.

Something about the woman's appearance deeply disturbs the mountaineer. For two paragraphs, he describes her in an increasingly grisly manner. He refers to her as a "living skeleton" and essentially describes her as being desiccated and almost mummified looking. He states, "Yet, there was a fascination in her very hideousness that kept my gaze fixed upon her." He goes on to compare her to a corpse risen from the grave, imagining the smell of mold and slime on her. As he recoils, he becomes aware that her eyes never leave the old man walking with him.

Just then, the tension is broken by the piercing cry of a panther emerging from the nearby woods, likely in search of its missing cub. The old woman seems unfazed, but the mountaineer is paralyzed with fear. Suddenly, the old man springs into action as the large panther emerges from the trees. The old man draws a knife and charges the panther. The panther, caught by surprise by the sudden charge, springs up into a tree and out onto a branch, preparing to pounce down from above. Turning toward the old woman, the old man rushes forward, snatches the cub and proceeds to bash it on the rocks until it is dead. Angrily, the panther leaps from the tree and falls short of the old man, who raises his knife again, preparing to fight. Suddenly, an even more disturbing shriek emerges from the old woman, who rushes between the two and locks eyes with the panther. The fierceness of the animal suddenly fades, and it runs off into the woods.

As the mountaineer stands there stunned, the old woman turns to the old man and says:

> I never saw you before. But I know you well. You are the human devil who murdered your promised bride at the White Rocks. And you shall know me. I am Moll Derry, the Fortune Teller. People call me the Witch of the Mountains. I saved you from the panther. Too easy and quick a death that would have been. I wish, before you die, to twist my fingers among your heart strings.

The man's head drops, and he shivers. Derry quickly proceeds to tell him that every night among these trees walks the bloodied ghost of Polly Williams. Every night her screams for mercy can be heard. The man then drops to his knees and buries his face in the dead leaves scattered on the ground. Moll Derry goes on to ask him why he always feels drawn to this spot even though he wants to turn back. She says, "You are here to meet your death. It is near. This night your ghost will face that of the beautiful girl who loved and trusted you so well. False lover, seducer, murderer, look up and see your doom."

The mountaineer sees the man raise his anguished face, saying that "all the agonies of hell" were pictured on it. Just then, the panther darts back out of the woods and latches onto the man's throat. He closes his eyes to avoid looking at the gruesome scene, and when he opens them, both the panther and Derry are gone. All that remains is the bloody corpse of the elderly Philip Rogers.

Even though the "Mountaineer's Tale" is fictional, it encapsulates the beliefs about Derry that were prevalent by the early twentieth century. She is identified as both a fortune teller and a witch and seems to have some power over the local wildlife. Using her abilities, she avenges Polly Williams (when the law did nothing) by tormenting Rogers and causes his death by luring out the panther. Even though it is set many years after the murder, it provides a feeling of justice for those familiar with the real story. Once again, Old Moll is labeled a witch but uses her power against a murderer.

This brings us to the final legend that Moll Derry is associated with, that of the Lost Children of the Alleghenies. Like the story of Polly Williams, this legend is based in fact, and the story has been repeated for a century and a half throughout Pennsylvania and beyond. Today one can visit a monument where the Cox children were found near Pavia in Bedford County. Folk singer Alison Krauss even recorded a song about the boys' tragic disappearance and Jacob Dibert's prophetic dreams called "Jacob's Dream." The most recent account was written by Michelle Bertoni and appeared in *Supernatural Lore of Pennsylvania: Ghosts, Monsters and Miracles*. While the story of the Lost Children is fascinating and could easily fill a book by itself, for our purposes, we are concerned only with the appearance of the witch, Moll Wampler. Wampler is not an essential part of the tale and is often left out of the retellings. Still, her appearance is an interesting tangent to the story that reflects some common beliefs about the supernatural. But is Moll Wampler really Moll Derry? The answer to that is a definitive no. As we have seen, Derry died long before 1856. That leaves us asking the question, who is Moll Wampler? And how did she become confused with Moll Derry? As it turns out, "Moll Wampler" might not even be Moll Wampler.

THREE WITCHES

The earliest mention in a historical account of a witch being consulted to locate the Lost Children of the Alleghenies appears to be Charles McCarthy's 1888 book *The Lost Children of the Alleghenies and How They Were Found Through a Dream*. It is possible that earlier accounts may exist, but they were not circulated outside the immediate area to the extent of McCarthy's volume. In his preface, McCarthy emphasizes that he has compiled a true and accurate account of the search for the boys and empathizes with the parents and searchers. He also had access to those who remembered and participated in the search for the boys. At sixty pages, the volume presents a detailed record of the incident.

The witch appears in chapter 4, titled "The Superstitious Hunters and the Witch." After almost a week of searching, the situation had become desperate, and even though the Cox family did not practice folk magic and were "opposed to all forms of sorcery, magic, or necromancy," many of the searchers did believe in its power. However, before they consulted the witch, they turned to a local dowser. Near Morrison's Cove lived a black man who had a reputation for locating things by practicing dowsing (sometimes called water-witching when used to locate sources of water). Using a forked peach tree branch, the man attempted to locate the Cox boys in the woods by letting the branch guide him. He was unsuccessful, leading McCarthy to (probably unfairly) label him a fraud.

Even though the dowser failed, some of the searchers were not ready to give up on a supernatural solution. McCarthy continued:

There was an old witch living in Somerset County who was noted for her conjuring power, not surpassed perhaps by the witch of Endor. After holding a consultation, it was determined by a few of the superstitious to send for her. The old lady, on arriving at the mountain, went through a number of mysterious conjuring tricks, after which she said she knew where the children were; she could see them plainly—that they were far out in the interior of the mountain, living and subsisting well on chestnuts that had lain on the ground over winter. She said that they lodged at night on a nice bed of leaves under a heavy bunch of laurel that protected them from the rain and snow.

This was immediately followed by a request for money by the witch. She told them that she could lead them to the children and that they would be safe by ten o'clock the next morning. Staggering on through the night, with a growing crowd of curious onlookers, the old woman led the searchers through the woods. Hours passed, and so did her promised deadline of ten o'clock. The witch continued to promise that they would be found soon. More hours passed with no clues as to the boys' location, and finally the witch herself could go no farther. In fact, she had become lost and would not have been able to find her way back out of the woods without the help of

This depiction of Susanna and Samuel Cox hangs in the Bedford County Historical Society. *Courtesy of Joe and Michelle McAndrew.*

The grave marker for Jacob Dibert at the Mt. Zion Reformed Church. *Courtesy of Joe and Michelle McAndrew.*

those who had sought her help. Those involved in procuring the witch's help were embarrassed that they had put their faith in her methods. While the book continues, discussing Jacob Dibert's dream and the fate of the children, the witch makes no further appearance.

Two things are noticeably missing from this account. First is the name of Moll Wampler. Instead, the reader is only told of a well-known witch from Somerset County. The second is any mention of an Erdspiegel. The divination method of the witch is not discussed in any detail at all. So when did Wampler and the Erdspiegel become part of the story? As it turns out, Moll Wampler actually makes her first appearance seven years earlier in a story by Frank Cowan in his 1881 book *An American Story-Book: Short Stories from Studies of Life in Southwestern Pennsylvania.* The problem is that, even though it appeared earlier, Cowan's story is fiction that is loosely based on the story of the Lost Children and one other missing child case.

Cowan's name has been mentioned several times in this text, as he was a local historian, writer and politician from Greensburg. He was born in 1844 and lived to 1905. Having a lifelong interest in Vikings, and being a bit of a prankster, Cowan once created a famous hoax that Viking burials had been found along the Potomac River. Later he would be responsible for the creation of Mt. Odin Park in Westmoreland County. Cowan was also interested in documenting the folklore and history of southwestern Pennsylvania, or the "Little World," as he liked to call it. His descriptions of witchcraft in the context of the Little World were likely the origin of a nickname sometimes associated with Moll Derry—"The Witch of the Little World."

Even though some of his writings were nonfiction, *An American Story-Book* declares itself to be fiction in the very first line. However, much like *The White Rocks*, it is fiction inspired by the culture and stories of the region. Generally, Cowan takes more liberties with his stories and the historical details than Hill did in his volume.

Moll Wampler appears in a short story in the middle of the book called "The *Erdspiegel*." Essentially, it is a story of two lost children, a boy and a girl, who disappeared walking home from school. They lived on their family farm on one of the ridges of Laurel Hill. When their dog, which usually accompanied them to school and back, returned bloodied and died on the doorstep of the farm, the parents knew something terrible had happened. They retraced the blood trail and determined that a wild animal had attacked, but the dog probably kept it distracted long enough for the children to flee into the woods and hide. This, of course, led to a search that went on for days without success. Some of the searchers decided it would be best to enlist the help of a local witch to find the children, so they set off for the home of Moll Wampler. She is described as follows:

Moll Wampler was a woman about sixty-five years of age, heavy and hunched about the shoulders, as bald as an egg: the skin, of her broad face and round head, tawny-yellow blotched and brown; her eyes small and bright, and brown as a new-born May-beetle; a great hairy mole on her short upper lip; and in her upper jaw two long yellow canine teeth that projected somewhat over her lower lip—great prong-like teeth that, with her round head and hunched form, might suggest, so forcibly to a naturalist, a walrus, that he could not look into her face without seeing the characteristic features of the sea-cow of the arctics. She was known for many miles as "the witch of the mountains." It was believed that she could ride on a broomstick through the air—yet she always hobbled along with a crutch and a cane on the ground; she could cure, with roots and herbs she alone knew, all diseases—yet her limbs were crooked and stiff and her fingers knobbed and knotted with rheumatism; she had the most unlimited power over the persons and possessions of others—yet she could not straighten her ugly, crooked back, while she lived in absolute destitution in a hovel!

It is clear how this description would influence later descriptions of Moll Derry that made her sound more hag-like. This is also, as far as can be determined, the first mention of her actually flying through the air on a broomstick. These elements were reflected in George Swetnam's accounts in the twentieth century, even though it is clear (to us) that Wampler and Derry could not be the same person. It seems that Swetnam never knew the date of Derry's death.

After the description of Moll Wampler herself, the story continues by describing the Erdspiegel, or earth-mirror. The text states, "By looking in this mirror, she could see anything in the earth, gold, silver, hidden treasure, or water; and, by an easy extension, anything on the earth, person, house or tree." It is through the power of the Erdspiegel that the children could be located, or at least, that is what some of the searchers believe. The Erdspiegel itself, as described earlier, is a special looking glass placed at the bottom of a black bag. When a witch peered inside, it would function like a crystal ball. In this story, the witch is taken to the mountain to perform her divination and lead the searchers to the children. After searching fruitlessly, the witch and her party cross paths with the desperate and distraught father. Thinking that she might have bewitched his children, he flies into a rage and begins to choke her. The witch then threatens him with a hex, and he lets go. He expects that the men with the witch might shoot him, but they do not, so he quickly snatches their basket of food to sustain himself and runs off to keep searching for his children. A little later in the story, Wampler attempts to mount an old horse because she was having trouble walking, but the horse becomes spooked because it could sense her magic and charges off into the forest, taking the old woman with her. The searchers give up and do not succeed in tracking her down. The search for the children is eventually called off, too, and they are not recovered. However, the following spring, the "half-crazed" father is out in the woods, sitting on a log, when he catches a glint of sunlight reflecting off something in the woods. He walks closer and realizes that it is the Erdspiegel, lying on the remains of Moll Wampler's body. As he picks it up, something else catches the farmer's eye. Just a few feet away from Wampler's body are two small skeletons. It seems that the Erdspiegel had found the children after all, and the farmer and his wife finally have closure.

One can see the variations in fact from the true story of the Lost Children of the Alleghenies. This leaves us unable to determine how much truth exists in the description of Moll Wampler. We cannot even be sure if Moll Wampler was the real name of the witch who was called to help with the

Lost Children or if that witch really used an Erdspiegel. Though there were several women named Wampler alive in Bedford County in the 1850s, there is no proof that any of them was considered a witch. Any oral sources that were available to Cowan are gone.

When one examines the sources, it is clear that George Swetnam is the one who claimed that there was a definitive link between Moll Derry and Moll Wampler. In *Devils, Ghosts, and Witches: Occult Folklore of the Upper Ohio Valley*, Swetnam states, in reference to Derry, that "her name is given as 'Moll Wampler,' perhaps out of concern for the feelings of surviving members (if any) of the Derry family." This statement confirms that Swetnam actually had very little information about the historical Moll Derry, who died before the Lost Children were even born and had many descendants. Swetnam also fails to grasp the geographic distance involved. One old woman would not be wandering across three counties on foot. He goes on to quote large sections of "The *Erdspiegel*" from *An American Story Book* directly as if it were a historical account. Just before that, however, he mentions in his introduction that an old local history book mentioned that a "conjurer or enchantress" was brought in from Somerset County to help in the search. We have seen the mention of the witch from Somerset County before, in Charles McCarthy's book on the Lost Children. Somerset was the home of the unnamed witch in his historical account. Luckily, we do know the name of the Somerset witch—Moll Dell.

Moll Dell was yet a third witch whom Swetnam confused with Moll Derry. He believed that it was another of her aliases. In the beginning of the Moll Derry section of *Devils, Ghosts, and Witches*, Swetnam wrote, "The most famous witch of the Little World was Moll Derry, or Dell, of whom for half a century many tales were told." But Moll Dell was a different person entirely. There is even less historical information about her than Moll Derry, but there are a couple of sources. One of them is Frank Cowan's *Southwestern Pennsylvania in Song and Story*. In a section titled "1838—Moll Dell," Cowan describes the reputation of the mysterious woman:

> *So great was the belief of the people of Somerset County in the supernatural powers of this old woman, that, in the generalizing language of my informer, she kept a whole township digging for a gold mine for a lifetime—till the excavations made looked like an incompleted railroad struck by lightning!*

Dell was well known for her ability to find things such as gold, which also explains why she may have been consulted in the search for the Lost

Children. It appears that she did use an Erdspiegel because it is referenced in a poem about her. The context of the creation of the poem and the identity of its author is not clear, but it is included here because it gives insight as to her somewhat sinister reputation:

A Witch! And lo! The simulacrum of
The Soul of Science melts into a mist
That sinks upon the soil of Somerset;
The circle of the sorcerer surrounds
The Little World of Appalachia;
The sun's obscured; the moon awry and monstrous;
The earth is the abode of newts and bats,
The baleful hemlock, jimson weed, and rhus;
A Brief von Gott hangs on the cabin's wall
To save from fire and thieves and pestilence;
The mirror of the screened Erdspiegel tells
Of the unknown within the earth and air;
The forked crutch of hazel and of peach
Sinks wells for oil and water by the thousand;
The sacred symbol of the yoni hangs
Above the doorway, in the horseshoe's form,
To save the inmates of the hall and hovel
From every evil influence and harm
That might attend an angry witch's charm—
The human heart, within the name Moll Dell,
Is rotten in the grave of sin—in hell!

On the surface, Moll Dell is portrayed in a more sinister manner than early accounts of Moll Derry. The poem contains references not only to the Erdspiegel but also to other protective forms of folk magic like a horseshoe above the door and a "*Brief von Gott.*" Also known as a Himmelsbrief, or "Letter from Heaven," a Brief von Gott was a copy of a letter that supposedly drifted down from heaven promising protection to its bearer. There were several different types of these that were popular in Germany and Pennsylvania, and they were passed along and copied like early chain letters. The line about the forked crutch of hazel and peach is a reference to divining or dowsing rods and water witching. As a whole, the poem portrays Somerset as a place thoroughly immersed in the beliefs of folk magic and witchcraft, with Moll Dell representing the most fearsome witch in the county.

An example of a Himmelsbrief, or letter from heaven, that circulated in Pennsylvania in the 1800s. *Author's collection.*

In a footnote to the poem, meant to explain the mention of the Erdspiegel, Cowan cites an interesting case that may have actually had as much influence on his fictional short story "The *Erdspiegel*" as the tale of the Lost Children of the Alleghenies. His footnote appears as follows:

> *The Erdspiegel, or witch's looking glass, is still in use among the superstitious in Southwestern Pennsylvania. In 1875, a little boy named Ankeny was lost on the Laurel Hill, east of Ligonier, when a witch of Somerset County, who had in her possession an Erdspiegel, was sent for, that she might see exactly where he was and direct aright the hundreds who had gathered from far and near to the scene of distress on the mountain. Upon her arrival, she looked into her glass concealed in the bottom of a black bag; but the presence of an unbeliever in the throng so beclouded the mirror that the child has not been seen to this day.*

Unfortunately, no further information on the disappearance of the Ankeny boy has been located at this point. Perhaps in the future new sources will be discovered. What this case does show is that it was more common to seek the help of a witch or folk magic practitioner when someone was lost than one might expect. Whether by using an Erdspiegel or some other form of divination, the witch provided an alternative method of searching when traditional methods were not successful. The situation is similar to the occasional use of psychics by police departments today when cases have gone cold. Even though there is no proof that Moll Dell was the witch in the 1875 case, she could still be the actual witch who was asked to look for the Lost Children in 1856.

Luckily, we have another source about the mysterious Moll Dell. She appeared in a newspaper article discussing another colorful local character from Somerset County. On May 29, 1895, Dr. T.F. Livingston wrote an article about the exploits of a highly skilled but eccentric local axe maker and metalsmith named "Axie" Yoder. The stories recounted in the article all took place before the Civil War, which would place them in the same period that Moll Dell was active. The witch appears about halfway through the article, where it is mentioned that she was in possession of an Erdspiegel that she could use to "see through the various strata of the earth and to discover hidden treasure and gold, as well as the baser metals." She would use her Erdspiegel to convince Yoder that she could help him find Braddock's lost gold.

The legend of Braddock's Gold has a long history in western Pennsylvania and Maryland. General Edward Braddock was sent to drive the French out of Fort Duquesne at the forks of the Ohio (present-day Pittsburgh) in 1755 at the start of the French and Indian War. Even though he had a superior force, he was defeated by the small French force and their Indian allies who used the terrain to their advantage. Since the defeat, rumors have circulated that the expedition's gold and Braddock's personal money were buried somewhere along the route (either before or after the battle). Local treasure hunters have searched for it ever since. (For more details on Braddock's Gold see the book *Legends and Lore of Western Pennsylvania*.)

Yoder and his associates hired Moll Dell to guide their search for the treasure. She gave him specific instructions on where to dig along Pine Run and how deep to go to find the box that contained the treasure. After they had surpassed the level in which they expected to find the chest, they returned to Dell to see what went wrong. She instructed them that they had dug too deep and that the Erdgeist, or earth spirits—basically gnomes—had moved the treasure. There were a dozen of these gnomes guarding the treasure according to Dell, and they had moved the treasure a quarter of a mile away. Axie Yoder packed up his equipment and moved to the new site to dig there. After a few weeks, Moll Dell reappeared and announced that she had a new vision. The trunk that they were currently digging for contained only $3,000 worth of silver. However, the main trunk, containing $200,000 worth of gold, was buried directly across the creek. It would take longer to retrieve this gold because it was so deep, and they would have to dig for nine months and nine days. Hearing this, Yoder again packed up his things, and he and his men moved across the run.

Sketch of Moll Dell instructing Axie Yoder and his men where to dig for Braddock's Gold. *Courtesy of Tom J. White.*

Months later, once a large pit was excavated, Moll Dell appeared again with her Erdspiegel, this time accompanied by her son Bill. She informed Yoder that he was within a few feet of the trunk and that he should arm his men as a precaution—and not just against human thieves. She said that the Erdgeist and dragons would fight to protect the gold, so the men had to use special silver bullets. They had to be "cooled in the blood of a black cat," because normal bullets would be ineffective. Interestingly, one of Yoder's helpers reported that shortly before Moll Dell arrived, the bottom of the pit filled with toads, snakes and lizards. As the men stood guard, there was a loud commotion in the trees, and one of them dodged to escape one of the dragons—reported as having wings larger than eagles—injuring himself in the process. At the same time, Moll Dell descended into the pit and personally instructed the men where to dig. Axie Yoder could hardly contain his excitement, and the men finally struck a large boulder. Dell confirmed that the treasure was under the boulder.

As the men were trying to move the boulder, Bill Dell's axe pick broke, causing him to swear loudly. (Bill Dell was Moll Dell's son.) Almost immediately, there was the sound that was compared to thousands of nails dropping fifty feet onto a tin surface. Then there was a shrill screech or scream that caused everyone to recoil (attributed to the Erdgeist). The gnomes had taken the treasure again, at least according to Moll Dell. One of the men was so angry that he was going to shoot Bill Dell for disturbing the Erdgeist, and he had to be restrained. The venture had cost Yoder over $1,000 by that point. Instead of learning his lesson, he supposedly continued searching without the help of Moll Dell.

The article portrays Moll Dell as a con woman, but her predictions and beliefs were not questioned by those seeking the gold because they shared in a supernatural worldview. Not everyone agreed with this assessment of Axie Yoder though. In February 1898, an article written by W.H. Welfley ran in the same paper as a response to the previous article. Welfley claimed that Yoder was a very advanced metalsmith whose activities were associated with magic by ignorant local farmers who did not understand his methods. He claimed that Yoder never consulted Dell, and his excavations were attempts to find ore. He actually spent only $195 in his search. (In spite of this, it is important to remember that many Pennsylvania German miners would try magical means in addition to scientific ones.) A few days later, a third article appeared, written by "Uncle Joe," an author who frequently wrote about county history and folklore. His article took a middle course, saying that while Yoder was indeed a very advanced metalsmith, he was a friend of his father's and he remembered many conversations between the two about lost treasure, the Erdgeist and the supernatural. His father even tried to convince him not to take such things so seriously. It is possible that Yoder used the search for ore as a cover story to hide his search for gold. Uncle Joe also mentioned Moll Dell in the article and added that even though she did not die in Somerset, there was a spring named after her where she used to stop and rest while walking the mountain.

None of the three articles questions the existence of Moll Dell or her Erdspiegel. Our sources on her are limited, but it is very likely that she was the old woman brought in from Somerset to help locate the Lost Children in Bedford. If so, Moll Wampler may not have actually existed at all. Then again, Wampler may have been the name of the witch who assisted in the 1875 case with the missing Ankeny boy. Again, we do not have enough information to know for sure one way or another. What we do know is that neither of these witches was Moll Derry.

REVEALING THE WITCH

In the mid-twentieth century, George Swetnam unintentionally combined the stories of Moll Derry, Moll Dell and Moll Wampler to create our modern legend of the Witch of the Monongahela. Some historical resources were less accessible when he was writing, and he did not fully comprehend the prevalence of the belief in witchcraft and folk magic in early western Pennsylvania. This accidental misidentification obscured not only the real story of Mary Derry but also that of Moll Dell and Moll Wampler (if she really existed). In Swetnam's defense, the legends and stories that he encountered were already vague, and some blended fact and fiction. In the 1800s, there was little attempt to document folk magic and similar folk beliefs in any academic sense. These beliefs were viewed merely as a curiosity or were discussed to show how backward some early settlers were and how far the industrializing scientific world had come. Of course, that was not an accurate assessment, as belief in folk magic and the supernatural continues to this day.

As we have explored her life and legends, Moll Derry seems to have left us with more questions than answers. In death, as in life, she remains a mystery. We cannot definitively say that she cursed the three hanged men or warned Polly Williams, even though substantial parts of the legends are based on facts. It does not necessarily mean that they did not happen but rather that they cannot be proven to have occurred. However, there are a few things that we can say with some certainty about Old Moll. It seems that she was primarily known for her skills at divination. One might argue that the nickname "Fortune Teller of the Revolution" is more appropriate than the label of witch. Divination is the one thing that is consistently associated with her in every account, historical or otherwise. Her methods may vary in the different accounts, but she was always sought out to reveal unseen things. Most people who wanted her help in those early days of Fayette County did so for this very reason. It seems as if some substantial stories about Moll Derry may be lost as well. How did she originally get the nickname of Fortune Teller of the Revolution? Was it a vision of the future that led her and her husband to change sides during the war? There must have been some legend behind it, something that earned her reputation in her youth, but it is lost to us now. We have no way of knowing how many people came to her over the years in a desperate effort to find lost belongings, animals or even a loved one. Still we cannot ignore the darker side of the eccentric woman in the mountains.

Whether Moll Derry actually practiced witchcraft or not, there were at least some people who thought her abilities came from a diabolical source, as evidenced in "The Mountain Hunter" article. This may stem from the belief held by many of her religious contemporaries that any type of folk magic came from the devil. Whether Derry actually cursed three men to hang or whether her apprentice slowly killed another, what matters is that people believed she was capable of it. And of course, if the article about the "Black Gang" was in fact correct, Ned Cassidy approached her to procure poison. That is not a service that a normal fortune teller would provide. While we have sadly lost the numerous personal accounts of interactions with Old Moll that were transmitted orally, we can reasonably infer that not everyone had pleasant interactions with her. As time passed, the merging of the stories about Moll Dell and Moll Wampler made Derry appear even more hag-like and dangerous.

Interestingly enough, Derry never really becomes the villain in any of the stories that are most commonly told about her. She is feared and her power respected (aside from the three hanged men who mocked her), but she does not use magic against innocent people. The people she cursed were bad men and murderers. She warned a young woman about her impending death. She attempted to locate missing children (even though that was not actually Derry). Traditionally, witches threaten social order and cause problems in the community. Derry, on the other hand, seemed to provide a supernatural service to the community. Moll Derry inhabited a gray area—a liminal space—in southern Fayette County.

Both feared and needed, Derry was more like a hex doctor or witch master than a traditional witch, straddling the line between light and dark magic. Over time, the nuances of the folk magic tradition were lost on succeeding generations, and any use of folk magic became associated with witchcraft. Mary Derry, Fortune Teller of the Revolution, became Old Moll, Witch of the Monongahela.

THE TRAGIC CASE
OF RHODA DERRY

In 1904, Dr. George Zeller walked into the Adams County Almshouse in Illinois. It was a visit that he would not forget. In 1902, the progressive doctor had become the head of the Illinois Hospital for the Incurable Insane. (He disliked the name intensely because he did not believe that his patients were incurable, and eventually he succeed in having the name changed.) Part of his duties as the head of the new hospital was to inspect the almshouses that harbored patients with mental illness throughout the state. These almshouses often had horrible living conditions by modern standards and were underfunded and understaffed. Doctors at that time were only beginning to understand the true nature of mental illness. Zeller was looking to help patients who would benefit from being transferred to the new facility. What he found in Adams County was heartbreaking.

Zeller found himself staring at a woman who looked only half alive. Bent and twisted, suffering from numerous health problems, the woman had spent decades inside what was called a Utica Crib. The crib was a small enclosed bed, just like a baby crib, but sealed at the top. It was used to restrain patients who were deemed to be dangerous to others or themselves. The woman was first admitted to the almshouse in 1860 when she was twenty-six. She spent most of her time there restrained in the crib, which amplified the decline of both her mental and physical health. Now, at the age of seventy, she was released by the doctor and taken to the new hospital for treatment. He used her as an example to draw attention to the plight of the mentally ill and push for reforms in the system. She lived only two more years, but it was long enough to attract public attention. The woman's name was Rhoda Derry. She was Moll Derry's granddaughter.

Rhoda was the youngest daughter of Moll Derry's son Jacob. She had been born in Indiana and moved with the family to Illinois as a child. It is unlikely that she ever met her grandmother, but she would have been familiar with family lore regarding "Old Moll." Nothing in Rhoda's early years indicated that she would have problems. However, as she grew older, she fell in love with a local man whose mother disapproved of the relationship. There was an argument with the mother, who allegedly cursed Rhoda. Rhoda seemed to take the curse seriously. She began to talk about witches and witchcraft and claimed the devil—or, as she said, "Old Scratch"—himself was tormenting her. At one point, she even fired shots in the family house at invisible witches who had come to harass her. Eventually, her actions became too much for the family to handle, and she was sent to the almshouse.

While most people in the community had decided that she was suffering from some type of insanity, others knew of her family lineage and proposed a supernatural explanation. Rhoda was descended from a witch, so she and her family would pay for Old Moll's practice of the dark arts. Perhaps, they thought, Rhoda had even dabbled herself. Her ramblings about witches only encouraged such speculation. We cannot know for sure, but it is likely that family stories about Moll Derry probably had a significant effect on young Rhoda. When her mental illness manifested, stories and beliefs about witchcraft were prominent in her mind. Years later, when Rhoda became a national figure and the face of reform in mental institutions, the rumors of witchcraft surfaced again in the press. This time they were overshadowed by the horrible and definitely true stories that were emerging from the state institutions. If Rhoda were alive today, she would likely be diagnosed with schizophrenia and definitely receive humane treatment. Tragically, during her life, she was unable to escape the long shadow of the Witch of the Monongahela.

Appendix

CHARMS, REMEDIES AND INCANTATIONS

There are many charms, prayers and incantations that were used among folk healers in Pennsylvania (and in the Appalachians in general), and these existed in many variations. Here are some examples of common charms or "spells" that have been drawn from John George Hohman's *The Long Lost Friend*. It was first published in 1819, while Moll Derry was alive, though there is no evidence that she ever saw or used the book. However, these charms are a good example of the types used by German folk healers and powwowers in early Pennsylvania.

A PRECAUTION AGAINST INJURIES

Whosoever carries the right eye of a wolf fastened inside of his right sleeve, remains free from all injuries.

TO REMOVE BRUISES AND PAINS

Bruise, thou shalt not heat;
Bruise, thou shalt not sweat;
Bruise, thou shalt not run,
No more than Virgin Mary shall bring forth another son. +++

To Heal a Sore Mouth

If you have the scurvy, or quinsy too,
I breathe my breath three times into you,
+++

To Cure Fits or Convulsions

You must go upon another person's land, and repeat the following: "I go before another court—I tie up my 77-fold fits." Then cut three small twigs off any tree on the land; in each twig you must make a knot. This must be done on a Friday morning before sunrise, in the decrease of the moon unbeshrewdly. +++ Then over your body where you feel the fits you make the crosses. And thus they may be made in all cases where they are applied.

How to Make Cattle Return to the Same Place

Pull out three small bunches of hair, one between the horns, one from the middle of the back, and one near the tail, and make your cattle eat it in their feed.

How to Destroy a Tape Worm

Worm, I conjure thee by the living God, that thou shalt flee this blood and this flesh, like as God the Lord will shun that judge who judges unjustly, although he might have judged aright. +++

Security Against Mad Dogs

Dog, hold thy nose to the ground,
God has made me and thee, hound!
+++
This you must repeat in the direction of the dog; and the three crosses you must make toward the dog, and the words must be spoken before he sees you.

HOW TO TREAT A COW AFTER THE MILK IS TAKEN FROM HER

Give to the cow three spoonfuls of her last milk, and say to the spirits in her blood: "Ninny has done it, and I have swallowed her in the name of God the Father, the Son, and the Holy Ghost. Amen" Pray what you choose at the same time.

TO SPELL-BIND A THIEF SO THAT HE CANNOT STIR

This benediction must be spoken on a Thursday morning, before sunrise and in the open air:

"Thus shall rule it, God the Father, the Son, and the Holy Ghost. Amen. Thirty-three Angels speak to each other coming to administer in company with Mary. Then spoke dear Daniel, the holy one: Trust, my dear woman, I see some thieves coming who intend stealing your dear babe; this I cannot conceal from you. Then spake our dear Lady to St. Peter: I have bound with a band, through Christ's hand; therefore, my thieves are bound even by the hand of Christ, if they wish to steal my own, in the house, in the chest, upon the meadow or fields, in the woods, in the orchard, in the vineyard, or in the garden, or wherever they intend to steal. Our dear Lady said: Whoever chooses may steal; yet if anyone does steal, he shall stand like a buck, he shall stand like a stake, and shall count all the stones upon the earth, and all the stars in the heavens. Thus I give thee leave, and command every spirit to be master over every thief, by the guardianship of Saint Daniel, and by the burden of this world's goods. And the countenance shall be unto thee, that thou canst not move from the spot, as long as my tongue in the flesh shall not give thee leave. This I command thee by the Holy Virgin Mary, the Mother of God, by the power and might by which he has created heaven and earth, by the host of all the angels, and by all the saints of God the Father, the Son, and the Holy Ghost. Amen." If you wish to set the thief free, you must tell him to leave in the name of St. John.

ANOTHER WAY TO SPELL-BIND THIEVES

Ye thieves, I conjure you, to be obedient like Jesus Christ, who obeyed his Heavenly Father unto the cross, and to stand without moving out of my sight, in the name of the Trinity. I command you by the power of God and the incarnation of Jesus Christ, not to move out of my sight, +++ like Jesus Christ was standing on Jordan's stormy banks to be baptized by John. And furthermore, I conjure you, horse and rider, to stand still and not to move out of my sight, like Jesus Christ did stand when he was about to be nailed to the cross to release the fathers of the church from the bonds of hell. Ye thieves, I bind you with the same bonds with which Jesus our Lord has bound hell; and thus ye shall be bound; +++ and the same words that bind you shall also release you.

TO RELEASE SPELL-BOUND PERSONS

You horseman and footman, whom I here conjure at this time, you may pass on in the name of Jesus Christ, through the word of God and the will of Christ; ride ye now and pass.

AGAINST BURNS

Our dear Lord Jesus Christ going on a journey, saw a firebrand burning: it was St. Lorenzo stretched out on a roast. He rendered him assistance and consolation; he lifted his divine hand and blessed the brand; he stopped it from spreading deeper and wider. Thus may the burning be blessed in the name of God the Father, Son and Holy Ghost. Amen.

AGAINST EVERY EVIL INFLUENCE

Lord Jesus, thy wounds so red will guard me against death.

To Charm Enemies, Robbers and Murderers

God be with you, brethren; stop, ye thieves, robbers, murderers, horsemen, and soldiers, in all humility, for we have tasted the rosy blood of Jesus. Your rifles and guns will be stopped up with the holy blood of Jesus; and all swords and arms are made harmless by the five holy wounds of Jesus. There are three roses upon the heart of God; the first is beneficent, the other is omnipotent, the third is his holy will. You thieves must therefore stand under it, standing still as long as I will. In the name of God the Father, Son and Holy Ghost, you are conjured and made to stand.

A Charm Against Fire-Arms

Jesus passed over the Red Sea, and looked upon the land; and thus must break all ropes and bands, and thus must break all manner of fire-arms, rifles, guns, or pistols, and all false tongues be silenced. May the benediction of God on creating the first man always be upon me; the benediction spoken by God, when he ordered in dream that Joseph and Mary together with Jesus flee into Egypt, be upon me always, and may the holy + be ever lovely and beloved in my right hand. I journey through the country at large where no one is robbed, killed, or murdered—where no one can do me an injury, and where not even a dog can bite me, or any other animal tear me to pieces. In all things let me be protected, as also my flesh and blood, against sins and false tongues which reach from the earth up to heaven, by the power of the four Evangelists, in the name of God the Father, God the Son, and God the Holy Ghost. Amen.

To Charm Guns and Other Arms

The blessing which came from heaven at the birth of Christ be with me [*name*]. The blessing of God at the creation of the first man be with me; the blessing of Christ on being imprisoned, bound, lashed, crowned so dreadfully, and beaten, and dying on the cross, be with me; the blessing which the Priest spoke over the tender, joyful corpse of our Lord Jesus Christ, be with me; the constancy of the Holy Mary and all the saints of God, of the three holy kings, Casper, Melchior and Balthasar, be with me; the holy four Evangelists, Matthew, Mark, Luke and John, be with me; the Archangels St.

Michael, St. Gabriel, St. Raphael and St. Uriel, be with me; the twelve holy messengers of the Patriarchs and all the Hosts of Heaven, be with me; and the inexpressible number of all the Saints be with me. Amen.

Papa, R. tarn, Tetragrammaton Angel.
Jesus Nazarenes, Rex Judeorum.

A Charm to Gain Advantage Against a Man of Superior Strength

I [*name*] breathe upon thee. Three drops of blood I take from thee: the first out of thy heart, the other out of thy liver, and the third out of thy vital powers; and in this I deprive thee of thy strength and manliness.

Habits Massa Dante Lantien. I. I. I.

SELECTED BIBLIOGRAPHY

Archival Materials

Beryl Burchinel Collection. Pennsylvania Department, Uniontown Public Library.

Derry and Gates Families Genealogy, compiled by Joan Brown Derry. Pennsylvania Department, Uniontown Public Library.

Dr. George Swetnam Collection. Manuscript Group 5, Indiana University of Pennsylvania Special Collections and Archives.

Fayette County Court Records Volume One, 1784–1831. Pennsylvania Department, Uniontown Public Library.

George Swetnam Papers, 1999.0039. Library and Archives Division, Senator John Heinz Pittsburgh Regional History Center.

Articles

Arnold, J.O. "Superstitions Ingrained in Minds of Many Moderns." *Connellsville Daily Courier*, July 28, 1947.

Black, Esther. "Lawrence County Legends." *Keystone Folklore Quarterly* 7, no. 1 (1962): 37–40.

Bolen, Albert. "Mountaineer's Tale." *Morning Herald*, January 19, 1916.

Butler Citizen. "That Witch Case." November 26, 1879.

———. "Witchcraft in Indiana County." April 27, 1888.

Byington, Robert. "Powwowing in Pennsylvania." *Keystone Folklore Quarterly* 9, no. 3 (1964): 111–17.

Cambria Freeman. "The Other Day, Mrs. Carr…" October 24, 1867.

Connellsville Herald. "Somerset County Superstition." February 23, 1883.

Connellsville Keystone-Courier. "Some Superstitions That Frighten Foolish People." February 26, 1886.

Daily Standard. "An Old Hunter." May 1, 1879.

Davies, Owen. "The Nightmare Experience, Sleep Paralysis, and Witchcraft Accusations." *Folklore* 114, no. 2 (2003): 181–203.

Genius of Liberty. "A Couple Who Slew Wild Animal's about Haydentown in Early Days." January 1, 1891.

Harris, Sharon Woods. "Ghosts Not Always a Ghastly Tale." *Pekin Daily Times*, October 31, 2015.

Juniata Sentinel and Republican. "The Mountain Hunter." February 19, 1879.

Livengood, T.F. "Axie and the Other Argonauts." *Somerset Herald*, May 29, 1895.

Morning Herald–Evening Standard. "Polly Williams Tombstone Dedicated." September 20, 1972.

Somerset Herald. "More About Our Famous 'Axie.'" February 23, 1898.

———. "Uncle Joe Writes about Witches." November 23, 1892.

———. "Witches and Witchcraft." December 3, 1879.

Storey, Jerry. "Tragedy at White Rock." *Pittsburgh Tribune-Review*, August 6, 1995.

Trimble, Scott. "Last of the Vikings: Frank Cowan, Pennsylvania's Other Great Hoaxer and a Man Who Changed History." *Western Pennsylvania History*, Fall 2007.

Welfley, W.H. "The True Story of 'Axie' Yoder." *Somerset Herald*, February 16, 1898.

Wertz, Marjorie. "Irwin Woman Cherishes Memory of Grandfather She Knows Through Writings." *Pittsburgh Tribune-Review*, May 14, 2012.

Wiley, Samuel T. "The Black Gang." *Genius of Liberty*, July 14, 1881.

Zemba, Liz. "Librarian Chronicles History of Fayette County Executions." *Pittsburgh Tribune-Review*, June 28, 2015.

Books

Albert, George Dallas, ed. *History of the County of Westmoreland Pennsylvania*. Philadelphia: L.H. Everts & Company, 1882.

Aurand, A. Monroe, Jr. *The Realness of Witchcraft in America*. Harrisburg, PA: Aurand Press, 1942.

Baker, Jim. *The Cunning Man's Handbook: The Practice of English Folk Magic 1500–1900*. London: Avalonia, 2014.

Bilardi, Chris R. *The Red Church, or The Art of Pennsylvania German Braucherei*. Sunland, CA: Pendraig Publishing, 2009.

Bristow, Arch. *Old Time Tales of Warren County*. Meadville, PA: Tribune Publishing, 1932.

Cowan, Frank. *An American Story Book, Short Stories from Studies of Life in Southwestern Pennsylvania*. Greensburg, PA, 1881.

———. *Southwestern Pennsylvania in Song and Story: With Notes and Illustrations*. Greensburg, PA, 1878.

Davies, Owen. *Grimoires: A History of Magic Books*. Oxford, UK: Oxford University Press, 2009.

———. *Popular Magic: Cunning Folk in English History*. London: Hambledon Continuum, 2003.

Derry, D. Doc. *Rhoda: A Tragic and True Story of a Farmer's Daughter*. Wasilla, AK: Tanaka River Publishing, 2011.

Ellis, Franklin. *History of Fayette County, Pennsylvania: With Biographical Sketches of Its Many Pioneers and Prominent Men*. Philadelphia: L.H. Everts & Company, 1882.

Fischer, David Hackett. *Albion's Seed: Four British Folkways in America*. Oxford, UK: Oxford University Press, 1989.

Frear, Ned. *The Lost Children*. Bedford, PA: Frear Publications, 2002.

Games, Alison. *Witchcraft in Early North America*. Lanham, MD: Rowman & Littlefield Publishers, 2010.

Haden, James. *A History of Uniontown, the County Seat of Fayette County, Pennsylvania*. Akron, OH: New Werner Co., 1913.

Herr, Karl. *Hex and Spellwork: The Magical Practices of the Pennsylvania Dutch*. Boston: Weiser Books, 2002.

Hohman, John George. *Pow-Wows; or The Long Lost Friend*. Airville, PA: Yardbird Books, 1992.

Hufford, David. *The Terror That Comes in the Night: An Experience-Centered Study of Supernatural Assault Traditions*. Philadelphia: University of Pennsylvania Press, 1982.

Kriebel, David W. *Powwowing Among the Pennsylvania Dutch: A Traditional Medical Practice in the Modern World*. University Park: Pennsylvania State University Press, 2007.

McCarthy, Charles. *The Lost Children of the Alleghenies and How They Were Found Through a Dream*. Huntingdon, PA: Brethren's Publishing Company, 1888.

Milnes, Gerald C. *Signs, Cures & Witchery: German Appalachian Folklore.* Knoxville: University of Tennessee Press, 2007.

Newton, J.H., ed. *History of Venango County Pennsylvania.* Columbus, OH: J.A. Caldwell, 1879.

O' Hanlon-Lincoln, Ceane. *County Chronicles: A Vivid Collection of Fayette County, Pennsylvania Histories.* Chicora, PA: Mechling Bookbindery, 2004.

Orth, Richard L.T. *Folk Religion of the Pennsylvania Dutch: Witchcraft, Faith Healing, and Related Practices.* Jefferson, NC: McFarland & Company, 2018.

Shaner, Richard. *Hexerei: A Practice of Witchcraft Among the Pennsylvania Dutch.* Indiana, PA: A.G. Halldin, 1973.

Swetnam, George. *Devils, Ghosts, and Witches: Occult Folklore of the Upper Ohio Valley.* Greensburg, PA: McDonald/Sward Publishing, 1988.

————. *Pittsylvania Country.* New York: Duell, Sloan & Pearce, 1951.

Veech, James. *The Monongahela of Old.* Pittsburgh, PA, 1892.

White, Thomas, ed. *Supernatural Lore of Pennsylvania: Ghosts, Monsters and Miracles.* Charleston, SC: The History Press, 2014.

————. *Witches of Pennsylvania: Occult History and Lore.* Charleston, SC: The History Press, 2013.

Websites

Granato, Sherri. "The Legend of Fayette County, Pennsylvania Witch; Mary 'Mollie' Derry." https://guides.wikinut.com/The-Legend-of-Fayette-County%2C-Pennsylvania-Witch%3B-Mary-Mollie-Derry/11dadjhb

"Mary 'Old Moll' Derry." https://sites.google.com/site/derrysinamerica2/maryoldmollderry.

Phoenix, Rob. "Pennsylvania German Powwow: Faith Healing and Folk Magic Among the Pennsylvania Germans." https://braucher.webs.com.

INDEX

Witch of the Monongahela. *See*
    Derry, Moll
Woodbridgetown 84

Y

Yoder, "Axie" 101, 102, 103
Yoder, Don 28

Z

Zeller, Dr. George 109

ABOUT THE AUTHOR

Thomas White is the university archivist and curator of special collections in the Gumberg Library at Duquesne University. He is also an adjunct lecturer in Duquesne's History Department and an adjunct professor of history at La Roche University. White received a master's degree in public history from Duquesne University. Besides the folklore and history of Pennsylvania, his areas of interest include public history, American cultural history and the occult. He is the award-winning author of ten other books, including *Legends and Lore of Western Pennsylvania*, *Forgotten Tales of Pennsylvania*, *Ghosts of Southwestern Pennsylvania*, *Forgotten Tales of Pittsburgh*, *Forgotten Tales of Philadelphia* (coauthored with Edward White), *Gangs and Outlaws of Western Pennsylvania* (coauthored with Michael Hassett), *A Higher Perspective: 100 Years of Business Education at Duquesne University*, *Witches of Pennsylvania: Occult History and Lore*, *Supernatural Lore of Pennsylvania: Ghosts, Monsters and Miracles* (editor) and *Haunted Roads of Western Pennsylvania* (coauthored with Tony Lavorgne).

Visit us at
www.historypress.com